The Science and Math Bookmark Book

The Science and Math Bookmark Book

300 Fascinating, Fact-Filled Bookmarks

Kendall Haven
and
Roni Berg

1999
Teacher Ideas Press
A Division of
Libraries Unlimited, Inc.
Englewood, Colorado

Copyright © 1999 Kendall Haven and Roni Berg
All Rights Reserved
Printed in the United States of America

All the bookmarks contained in this book are original, created expressly for this publication, and are fully protected by copyright. Any resemblance to any design or picture from any other source is purely coincidental. Copies of the bookmarks may be made by the original purchaser of this book without special permission or additional reproduction fees. However, the bookmarks may not be used in whole or in part for resale either in printed or electronic form. Individual library media specialists and teachers may make copies of the bookmarks for classroom use in a single school. All the text in this book is protected by copyright and may not be reproduced, stored in a retrieval system, or transmitted, in any form or by any means, electronic, mechanical, photocopying, recording, or otherwise, without the prior written permission of the publisher.

TEACHER IDEAS PRESS
A Division of
Libraries Unlimited, Inc.
P.O. Box 6633
Englewood, CO 80155-6633
1-800-237-6124
www.lu.com/tip

Library of Congress Cataloging-in-Publication Data

Haven, Kendall F.
　The science and math bookmark book : 300 fascinating, fact-filled bookmarks / by Kendall Haven and Roni Berg.
　　xii, 115 p. 22x28 cm.
　　Includes index.
　　ISBN 1-56308-675-1 (softbound)
　　1. Science--Miscellanea. 2. Mathematics--Miscellanea. 3. Bookmarks. I. Berg, Roni. II. Title.
Q173.H375 1999
500--dc21   99-12426
                 CIP

CONTENTS

Introduction xi

PHYSICAL SCIENCES

Branches of the Physical Sciences 2
How Big Is the Universe? 2
The Sun 2
Planet Earth 3
Solar System Facts 3
How Far Is the Sun? 3
How Big Are the Planets in Our Solar System? 4
If the Sun Were a Beach Ball 4
Planetoid Factoids 4
Jupiter 5
Asteroids 5
Meteors and Meteorites 5
What Else Is in the Solar System? 6
What Is the Universe? 6
What Is the "Big Bang"? 6
What Is a Galaxy? 7
Milky Way Facts 7
What Are Stars? 7
Can a Star Die? 8
What's Left After a Star Dies? 8
Neutron Stars and Pulsars 8
Black Holes 9
Who Was First in Space? 9
First Animals in Space 9
Measuring Distance Among the Stars 10
How Close Are the Nearest Stars? 10
The Mighty Telescope 10
The Mysterious Moon 11
Element Facts 11
Acids and Bases 11
What Is pH? 12
Common Acids and Bases 12
Carbon 12
The Miracle of Salt 13
Atoms and Molecules 13
Some Common Molecules 13
What Is Inside an Atom? 14
Protons and Neutrons 14
The Temperature Scales 14
What Is Electricity? 15
"Natural" Electricity 15
Ben Franklin's Kite 15
Measuring Electricity 16
"Artificial" Electricity 16
Electricity and Magnetism 16

v

What Is Magnetism? 17
Nuclear Fission and Fusion..17
Why Does a Light Bulb Glow?..17
What Is a Transformer? 18
Semiconductors..18
Matter and Energy...18
Measuring Matter...19
Mass and Weight..19
Basic Physics Terms 19
What Is a Rainbow?...20
What Is Gravity?..20
The Four Forces of the Universe 20
What Is Friction?..21
What Is Light?..21
The Parts of the Frequency Spectrum 21
Lasers 22
How Does a Microwave Work?...22
Time Trivia 22
Time Terms 23
What Is Radioactivity?...23
Inorganic and Organic Chemistry 23
What Is an Explosion? 24
What Is the Scientific Method? 24
What Makes a Rocket Move? 24
What Is a Light Year? 25
Light Facts 25
Fluorescent and Luminescent Light...25
What Is Heat?...26
Comparing Temperature Scales 26
Fire 26
What Is a Vacuum?..27
Pressure and Pumps 27
What Makes an Airplane Fly and a Baseball Curve? 27
What Is a Comet?...28
Finding a Star 28
The Elements 28
The Periodic Table...29
Mixtures and Compounds 29
How Big Is an Atom? 29
How Does a Power Plant Create Electricity? 30
Types of Power Plants 30
How Does a Telephone Work? 30
The Timeline of Flight...31
Your Weight on Other Planets...31
Car Talk 31
The History of Rockets 32
Inventions Before 1800..32
Inventions Between 1800 and 1850...32
Inventions Between 1850 and 1900...33
Inventions Between 1900 and 1940...33
Inventions Between 1940 and 1980...33

Contents   vii

When Does a Full Moon Rise?...34
Copernicus...34
Galileo..34
Roger Bacon..35
Marie Curie..35
Joseph Priestly...35
Charles Goodyear..36
Thomas Edison..36
Wilhelm Roentgen..36

Earth Sciences

Branches of Earth Sciences..38
World's Longest Rivers...38
Waterfalls...38
Driest Places..39
Wettest Places...39
Northernmost, Easternmost..39
The Contiguous 48..40
The International Date Line..40
Caverns..40
Stalactites and Stalagmites...41
The Newest Land on Earth...41
The Lowest Places on Earth...41
Going Below Sea Level..42
The Highest Mountains...42
Highest U.S. Peaks...42
U.S. Mountain Ranges..43
Mountain Ranges of the World..43
Islands of the World..43
How Big Are the Oceans?..44
What's Hot? What's Not?...44
Hottest and Coldest...44
Natural Disasters...45
The Tropics..45
Glaciers..45
Glaciers During the Ice Ages...46
Inside the Earth...46
Rock Facts...46
Where Do Rocks Come From?..47
What Is a Mineral?..47
Measuring Geologic Time..47
Dating Ancient Rocks...48
Where Did the Atmosphere Come From?...48
Layers of the Atmosphere..48
What Is a Cloud?...49
Types of Clouds..49
How Much Does Air Weigh?...49
Humidity and Dew Point..50
What's in Air?..50
What Is Lightning?...50
What Is Thunder?..51
The Color of the Sky..51

Snowy Places 51
What Is Fog? 52
What Is Wind? 52
Windiest Places 52
Seas and Oceans 53
Naming the Seas 53
Straits, Bays, Gulf, Fjords, and Estuaries 53
What Is the Coastal Zone? 54
What Does SCUBA Stand For? 54
Where Do Beaches Come From? 54
Why Are Oceans Salty? 55
Major U.S. Estuaries 55
Waves 55
Why Do Waves Get Bigger and Break at the Beach? 56
How Deep Is the Ocean? 56
What Controls the Tides? 56
Tsunamis 57
Precipitation Words 57
What Is an Ice Age? 57
What Is a Continent? 58
The Water Cycle 58
Types of Rivers 58
Bodies of Fresh Water 59
Soil and Dirt 59
Polar Facts 59
What Is a Desert? 60
What Causes Ocean Currents? 60
Naming the Currents 60
What Are Tectonic Plates? 61
Ocean Plants 61
The Inter-Tidal Zone 61
Ocean Mammals 62
What's the Difference Between a Bay and an Estuary? 62
What's a Crustacean? 62
What's a Mollusk? 63
Ozone 63
Tornadoes 63
Typhoons, Hurricanes, and Cyclones 64
How Much Rain Falls Every Year? 64
What Is *El Nino*? 64

LIFE SCIENCES

The Branches of Life Science 66
Animal and Plants 66
How Do We Group Living Things? 66
What's in the Animal Kingdom? 67
What's in the Plant Kingdom? 67
What's in the Fungi and Single Cell Kingdoms? 67
What's Below a Kingdom? 68
Why Do We Classify Things? 68
How Many Animals Are There? 68
What Is Evolution? 69
Mythical Creatures 69

Plant Facts	69
The Biggest Things	70
U.S. Trees	70
Tree Tidbits	70
Tree Facts	71
Biggest Animals	71
Biggest Carnivores	71
Fastest Animals	72
The Mighty Insects	72
Shark Facts	72
Poisonous Things	73
Sleepy Animals	73
What Is an Ecosystem?	73
What Threatens Ecosystems?	74
What Is Life?	74
The Circulatory System	74
Blood	75
The Heart	75
Where Does the Blood Go?	75
The Nervous System	76
What Is a Neuron?	76
Brain Signals	76
The Nose Knows	77
The Brain	77
How You Hear	77
Why Two Ears and Two Eyes?	78
Your Body's Biggest and Smallest	78
Cell Facts	78
Inside a Cell	79
In the Nucleus of a Cell	79
Nutrition Quiz	79
The Mighty Muscles	80
The Digestive System	80
What Is a Liver?	80
Heart Attacks and Brain Attacks	81
Why Do Humans Sleep and Dream?	81
Amazing DNA	81
Nutrients	82
Vitamins	82
The Immune System	82
The Types of Blood	83
The Skeleton	83
What's in a Skeleton?	83
Tooth Talk	84
The Human Factory	84
The Biggest Dinosaurs	84
The Triassic Period	85
The Jurassic Period	85
The Cretaceous Period	85
Extinct Animals	86
Naming Groups of Animals	86
Grass Facts	86
Crocodiles and Alligators, Butterflies and Moths	87

Grass and Weeds, Horses and Zebras 87
Animal Transformations 87
The Parts of a Plant 88
Tree Trivia 88
The Parts of an Ecosystem 88
About Niches 89
What Is Diversity? 89
Are Forest Fires Good or Bad? 89
When One Part of an Ecosystem Is Destroyed 90
Where Does Pollution Come From? 90
What's in Our Garbage? 90
What's the Endangered Species List? 91
Dian Fossey 91
Charles Darwin 91
Louis Pasteur 92
Gregor Mendel 92
Jane Goodall 92

MATH

Zero—the Magic Number 94
The Seven Parts of the Number System 94
Why Were Numbers Developed? 94
What Is pi (π)? 95
What Is a Prime Number? 95
Number Bases 95
Roman Numerals 96
Fractions 96
Infinity 96
The World's Oldest Math Puzzle 97
Perfect Numbers 97
What Is an Equation? 97
Algebraic Symbols 98
A Magic Square 98
Two-Dimensional Shapes 98
Four-Sided Objects 99
Triangles 99
Conic Sections 99
Measuring Volume 100
What Is Algebra? 100
Finding the Area 100
Finding the Volume 101
Solving Equations 101
Computer Trivia 101
Metric and U.S. Measurements 102
Archimedes 102
Isaac Newton 102
Pierre de Fermat 103
Euclid 103
Sophie Germain 103
Sonya Kovalevsky 104
John Napier 104
Al Khwarizmi 104

Index 105

INTRODUCTION

Bookmarks have been in fashion since the early 17th century. Paper, cloth, ribbon, woven reeds, leather, silk, metal (e.g., gold, silver, copper, brass), and parchment have been used to mark a page either for future reference or to signal where the reader stopped. They have appeared in every culture that has printed words on paper pages.

The millions of bookmarks humans use have not been created just for decoration. By 1860, bookmarks sprouted advertisements for products such as soap, corsets, food, greeting cards, and medicines. Service announcements appeared by the 1890's promoting the offerings of insurance companies to book publishers. By 1920, public service announcements and promotions by nonprofit associations appeared on bookmarks.

If bookmarks can promote products while they mark a page, they can also educate. The bookmarks in this book are designed to support science education in a fun way by using fascinating facts to stimulate students' curiosity about major science concepts behind the facts. Science facts, concepts, and trivia have always intrigued us because they present amazing insights about the Earth, the matter and life of the Earth, the universe that surrounds it, and the history of each of these areas. What animal has the largest eyes in the world? A giant squid. Their eyes are as big as beach balls. Where are the three highest waterfalls in the United States? All three are in Yosemite Valley, California. What is the largest living thing on Earth? One of the giant sequoia trees in California, as big as 15 mammoth blue whales or 360 full-grown elephants! When you exercise, what percentage of your blood is diverted to support skeletal muscles? Just over half. Most of this blood is diverted from digestion and kidneys.

Kids love science facts. So do adults. These facts have a way of creeping into ordinary conversation to dazzle friends and co-workers.

This book of 300 math and science bookmarks combines the appeal of science facts and visually exciting graphics with the practicality of a bookmark. All three major divisions of science are represented: physical, earth, and life sciences. We focused on four prominent fields within each general category—for example, astronomy, chemistry, energy, and physics for physical sciences. Math entries are similarly divided into subgroups: the development of numbers, geometry, systems of calculation, and mathematical devices. Admittedly, there are some specific areas of science we did not cover. But our attempt was to provide interesting and important information in as many fields as possible.

Many of the bookmarks are formatted into quiz questions. We tried to make these questions both intriguing and challenging. Answers for all questions are included on the bookmark.

The information in this book was derived from over 100 science and math texts and reference books, and from extensive previous research by the authors. It represents the current state of scientific knowledge, theory, and thinking.

These bookmarks are intended to be copied and distributed in media centers, classrooms, public libraries, and homes. The back of each bookmark is available for personalized information (e.g., library hours and locations) or for follow-up questions, assignments, and information extending the factual information on the front side.

We would like to extend special thanks to Buzz Kellogg, Ph.D., the librarians at Sonoma State University, Toby Cowen, Jacqueline Keywood, Donna Clark, Karen Gibson, and Leslie Salmon-Zhu for lending their special touch to this book. We would also like to thank Mary Ann Bull (Forest Lake Elementary School in Enterprise, Florida), Christine Critchfield (Henderson School, Boca Raton, Florida), Marsha Goldsmith (Glen Burnie Elementary School, Glen Burnie, Maryland), and Linda Young (Beckly Elementary School, Las Vegas, Nevada) and their staffs for reviewing the content of the bookmarks.

Enjoy these bookmarks. See how much of this information you already knew. Use the bookmarks to launch related research projects, to introduce units, to thrill and impress your friends, or just to enjoy. Cut them out, copy them, distribute them, use them.

On your MARK, get set . . . CLIP!

Physical Sciences

What are the physical sciences, and what do they study?

Astronomy: space and the bodies in it.

Chemistry: the formation and properties of molecules, or combinations of atoms.

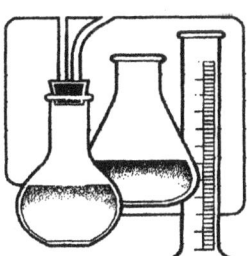

Physics: the study of matter and energy.

From *The Science and Math Bookmark Book*.
© 1999 Kendall Haven and Roni Berg.
Teacher Ideas Press. 1-800-237-6124

How big is the UNIVERSE?

Ans: We really don't know. The farthest distance ever measured is from earth to a quasar 13.2 billion light years away.

BUT, Earth isn't on one edge of the Universe. That quasar isn't on the other edge.

SO, the Universe has to be bigger than that. What's a good guess? 22 to 24 billion light years across (140,000,000,000,000,000,000,000 miles).

From *The Science and Math Bookmark Book*.
© 1999 Kendall Haven and Roni Berg.
Teacher Ideas Press. 1-800-237-6124

The Sun:

The sun is an ordinary, average-sized star.

Suns (stars) are really burning balls of gas (mostly hydrogen and helium).

At its center, the Sun is over 28,000,000°F.

At the surface it's a cool 9600°F.

Our sun will last another 5 billion years before it burns out.

From *The Science and Math Bookmark Book*.
© 1999 Kendall Haven and Roni Berg.
Teacher Ideas Press. 1-800-237-6124

Planet Earth

- Earth condensed from space junk 5 billion years ago.

- Earth's crust formed 4.5 billion years ago.

- Vapor condensed into water 4 billion years ago.

- Life (bacteria) formed 3.5 billion years ago.

- An oxygen/nitrogen atmosphere formed about 2 billion years ago.

- The first land plants grew 1.5 billion years ago.

Are all the planets the same?

Answer: No!

The inner four planets (Mercury, Venus, Earth, and Mars) are called "Terrestrial" planets because they formed as collections of solid matter.

The outer five (Jupiter, Saturn, Uranus, Neptune, and Pluto) are called "Jovian" because they all started as condensed balls of gas—like the Sun.

HOW FAR IS IT TO THE SUN?

PLANET	MILES
MERCURY	36,000,000
VENUS	67,200,000
EARTH	92,955,900
MARS	141,600,000
JUPITER	778,300,000
SATURN	887,000,000
URANUS	1,784,000,000
NEPTUNE	2,794,000,000
PLUTO	3,675,000,000*

*PLUTO DOESN'T TRAVEL IN A CIRCULAR ORBIT AROUND THE SUN AS THE OTHER PLANETS DO. SOMETIMES IT IS FARTHER AWAY THAN THIS. SOMETIMES IT IS CLOSER TO THE SUN THAN NEPTUNE IS.

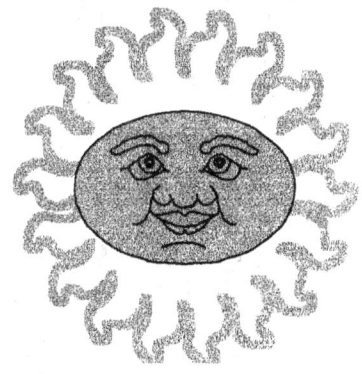

How big are the planets in our solar system?

The Sun is 865,036 miles across. Jupiter is 1/10 that size.

Earth is less than 1/100th that size. Earth's diameter = ?*

Granymede, the biggest moon of Jupiter, and Titan, the biggest moon of Saturn, are both bigger than the two smallest planets, Mercury and Pluto.

The solar system is mostly empty space. If you started at the middle of the sun and walked past Pluto, you'd be in empty space 99.99% of the time.

*Ans: 7,926 miles

How BIG is the stuff in the solar system?

If the Sun were a 12-inch beach ball, then:

- Mercury is a *Grape Seed* 164 feet away *(Can you draw a picture of each food?)*
- Venus is a *Pea* 284 feet away
- Earth is a *Lima Bean* 430 feet away
- Mars is a *Raisin* 654 feet away
- Jupiter is an *Orange* 1/2 mile away
- Saturn is a *Tangerine* 4/5 mile away
- Uranus is a *Plum* 1.1 miles away
- Neptune is a *Lime* 2.5 miles away
- Pluto is a *Grain of Rice* 3.0 miles away

On the same scale, the nearest star, Proxima Centauri, is a big beach ball 8,000 miles away! It's like having one beach ball in New York and another in Australia, with only empty space between.

Planetoid Factoids

—Pluto's year equals 248 Earth years; Neptune's year equals 165 Earth years; Uranus' equals 84. If you lived on any of the three outer planets, you probably wouldn't live long enough to have even one birthday!

—If there is life anywhere else in our solar system, it's probably frozen organic molecules on one of Jupiter's moons, not on Mars!

—Mars has crisscrossing red lines that look like engineered canals. People used to think Martians must have built them. But they're really natural channels formed by water and wind.

Jupiter, the biggest planet, rotates once every ten hours. Its surface, at the equator, travels 30 times as fast as Earth's.

The famous "red eye" of Jupiter is really a giant hurricane (bigger than all of north America) that's been raging for 1,000 years!

Jupiter is almost big enough to have the gravitational forces to become a star. It's 1/80 the necessary size—which in astronomical terms is pretty close.

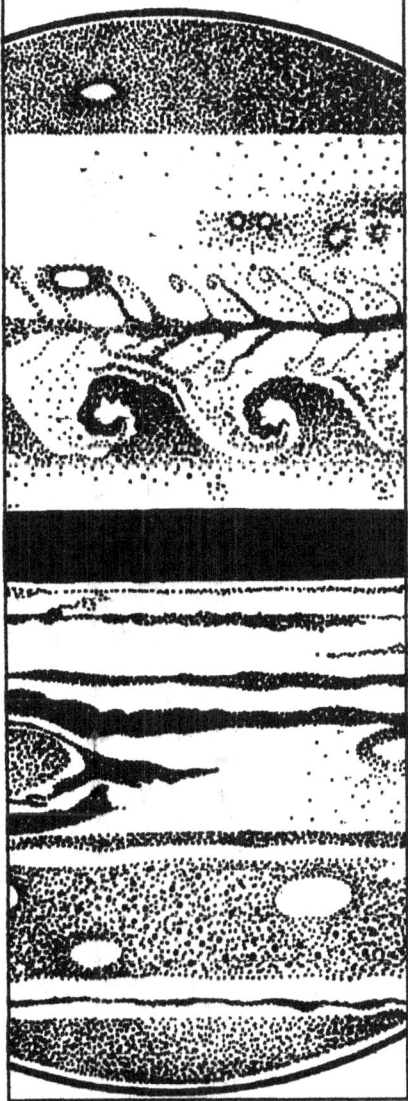

Asteroids

—Asteroids are concentrated in one ring around the Sun, called the asteroid belt.
—Over 45,000 "fragments of rock" orbit in this belt between Mars and Jupiter.
—Are they all small hunks of rock? No! The biggest are Ceres (582 miles across), Pallas (377 miles across), and Vesta (322 miles across).
—There are over 100 asteroids bigger than 100 miles across. Over five hundred have been named.

Meteors & Meteorites

• Bits of rock fall from space into our atmosphere all the time. They are called meteors. The Earth gains 20 tons of space junk every day.
• Shooting stars (meteors) are often no bigger than a grain of sand, but burn up very brightly as they fall.
• If it survives to hit the ground, it's called a meteorite.
• Most meteorites are tiny. But 120 have left big craters—ranging from 10 feet to a few hundred miles across.

Physical Sciences 6

BESIDES STARS, PLANETS, AND ASTEROIDS, WHAT ELSE IS IN THE SOLAR SYSTEM?

- **Solar wind**—radiation from the sun.
- **Space dust**.
- **8000+ satellites** and pieces of man-made junk in orbit around the Earth.
- **Radiation**—all kinds of radiation streams through our system.
- **Light** (photons).
- **Comets** (more than 20 loop around our sun).
- **Moons** (Earth, Jupiter, and Saturn have them).
- **Undiscovered floating stuff**—new hunks of rock are being discovered every year!

From *The Science and Math Bookmark Book*.
© 1999 Kendall Haven and Roni Berg.
Teacher Ideas Press. 1-800-237-6124

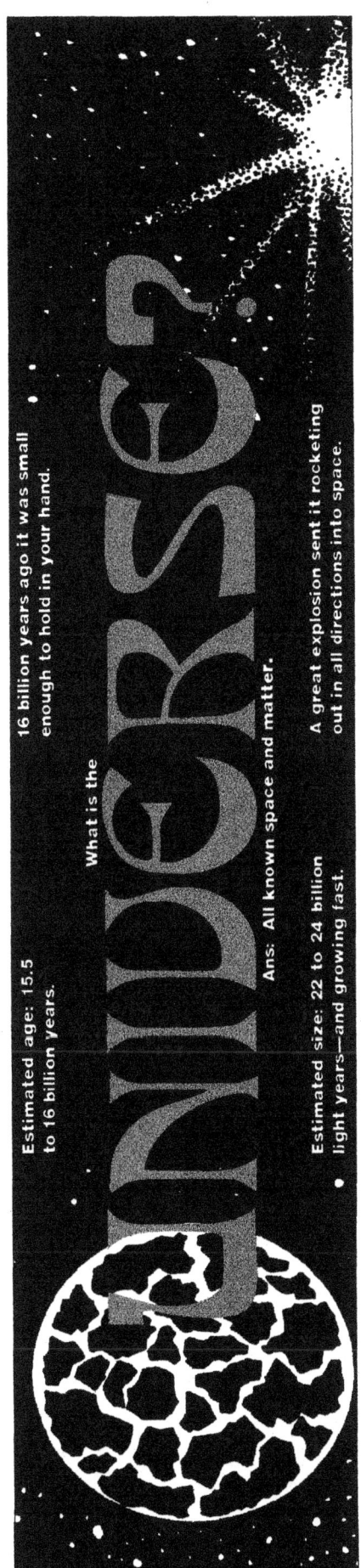

What is the UNIVERSE?

Estimated age: 15.5 to 16 billion years.

16 billion years ago it was small enough to hold in your hand.

Ans: All known space and matter.

A great explosion sent it rocketing out in all directions into space.

Estimated size: 22 to 24 billion light years—and growing fast.

From *The Science and Math Bookmark Book*.
© 1999 Kendall Haven and Roni Berg.
Teacher Ideas Press. 1-800-237-6124

What is the BIG BANG?

Ans: It is how we think the universe started.

It's still a theory. 16 billion years ago the entire universe was stuffed into one small ball. Then, BANG! It exploded. Matter was shot out in all directions. That was the beginning of our universe.

From *The Science and Math Bookmark Book*.
© 1999 Kendall Haven and Roni Berg.
Teacher Ideas Press. 1-800-237-6124

What is a galaxy?

Ans: All stars are clustered into large groups called galaxies—a few million to 500 billion stars in each.

There are three types of galaxies:

- Most are **Spiral** galaxies—like the Milky Way.

- Some are **ELLIPTICAL** galaxies—shaped like large ellipses.

- A few are **Irregular** galaxies—any other shape.

The biggest galaxy, called Abell 2020, is almost 20 times bigger than the Milky Way. It is 1.7 million light years away in Virgo.

The first galaxy was discovered in 1920 by Edwin Hubble.

FACTS

ABOUT OUR GALAXY

The Milky Way Galaxy

—is 100,000 light-years across.
—is 30,000 light-years thick.
—has 100 billion stars.
—is moving 170 miles-per-second away from the center of the universe.

Our sun is out near the galaxy's edge.

If the universe was one mile across, the Milky Way would be 1/100th of an inch wide.

What are Stars?

Ans: Cosmic gas and dust began to condense into clusters about 12-13 billion years ago. They are called stars.

—Stars are burning balls of hydrogen and helium gas squished together by tremendously powerful gravity.

—There is great variety in stars. If the Sun were a basketball, some stars would be no bigger than a grain of sand, and some would be bigger than an office building. They come in every color and brightness.

—The biggest known star is Alpha Orions, 500 times the size of our sun.

Can a star die?

★ YES AND NO.

★ EVENTUALLY A STAR BURNS THROUGH ALL ITS HYDROGEN, HELIUM, AND OTHER GASEOUS FUEL.

★ THEN ITS FIRES DIE AND THE STAR COLLAPSES.

★ THAT IS WHAT WE CALL THE DEATH OF A STAR.

★ BUT IT'S NOT REALLY DEAD. THERE IS STILL STAR MATTER LEFT.

What is left after a star dies?

Small and medium stars collapse into either Red Giants or more stable White Dwarfs. Both are small, cool shells of their former selves. (The names refer to the size and color of the planet-like body.)

Big stars can go supernova as they collpase. That's when the star tears itself apart in a giant explosion. What's left after a star goes supernova is either a neutron star, a pulsar, or a black hole.

What is a Neutron Star?

A Neutron Star is created from a supernova explosion so fierce, electrons are forced inside protons, creating all neutrons inside the atoms of the star. The resulting star is small (maybe ten miles across) but is so dense it has the same mass as our Sun, which is over 850,000 miles across!

Pulsars are rapidly spinning neutron stars (some as fast as 1000 revolutions a second). Pulsars are noticeable because hot spots on the surface emit radio waves that seem to pulse on and off as the pulsar spins.

Physical Sciences 9

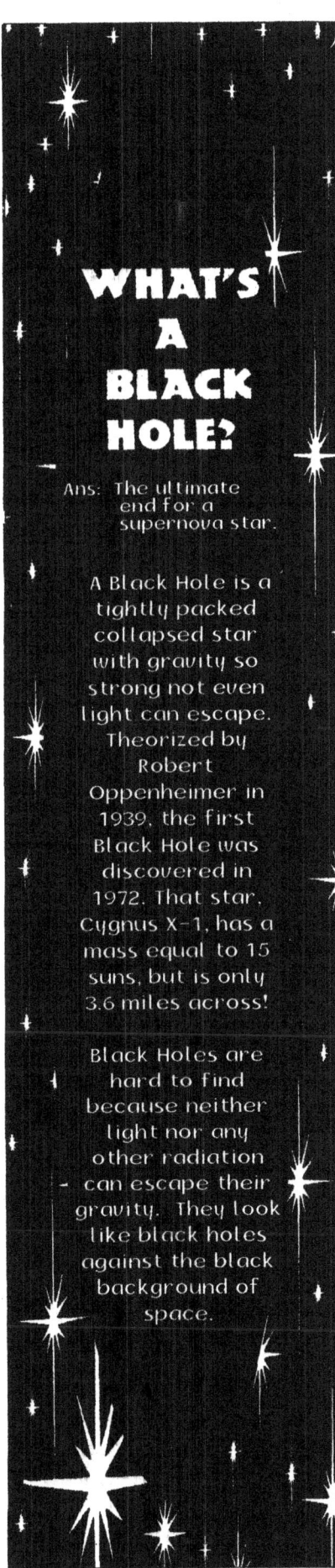

WHAT'S A BLACK HOLE?

Ans: The ultimate end for a supernova star.

A Black Hole is a tightly packed collapsed star with gravity so strong not even light can escape. Theorized by Robert Oppenheimer in 1939, the first Black Hole was discovered in 1972. That star, Cygnus X-1, has a mass equal to 15 suns, but is only 3.6 miles across!

Black Holes are hard to find because neither light nor any other radiation can escape their gravity. They look like black holes against the black background of space.

From *The Science and Math Bookmark Book.*
© 1999 Kendall Haven and Roni Berg.
Teacher Ideas Press. 1-800-237-6124

WHO WAS 1st IN SPACE?

1st satellite: *Sputnik 1* (USSR) on Oct 4, 1957.

1st U.S. satellite: *Explorer 1* on Jan 31, 1958.

1st human: Yuri Gagarin of the USSR on April 12, 1961.

1st American: John Glenn on Feb 20, 1962.

1st 10 humans in space: six from USSR and four from United States.

1st five countries in space (in order): USSR (1957), USA (1958), France (1965), Italy (1967), Australia (1967).

From *The Science and Math Bookmark Book.*
© 1999 Kendall Haven and Roni Berg.
Teacher Ideas Press. 1-800-237-6124

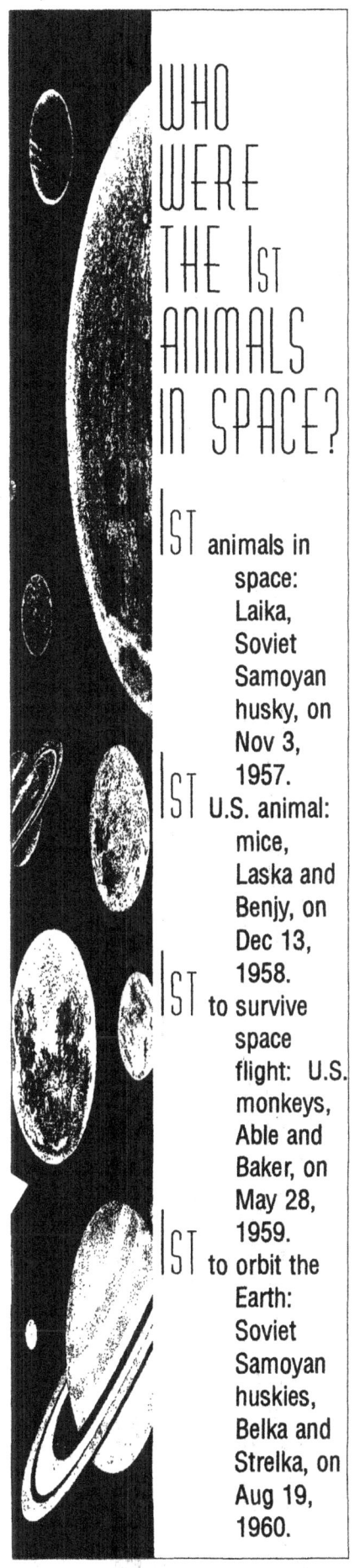

WHO WERE THE 1st ANIMALS IN SPACE?

1st animals in space: Laika, Soviet Samoyan husky, on Nov 3, 1957.

1st U.S. animal: mice, Laska and Benjy, on Dec 13, 1958.

1st to survive space flight: U.S. monkeys, Able and Baker, on May 28, 1959.

1st to orbit the Earth: Soviet Samoyan huskies, Belka and Strelka, on Aug 19, 1960.

From *The Science and Math Bookmark Book.*
© 1999 Kendall Haven and Roni Berg.
Teacher Ideas Press. 1-800-237-6124

MEASURING DISTANCE AMONG THE STARS

For nearby distances:
MILES—
(but even nearby stars are trillions of miles away).

For measurements around the solar system:
AU's
(Astronomical Units)—
1 AU equals the distance from Earth to Sun, or 92,955,900 miles.

For distances in space:
LIGHT YEARS—
1 Light Year equals the distance light travels in one year, or 5,875,000,000,000 miles; almost 6 trillion miles!

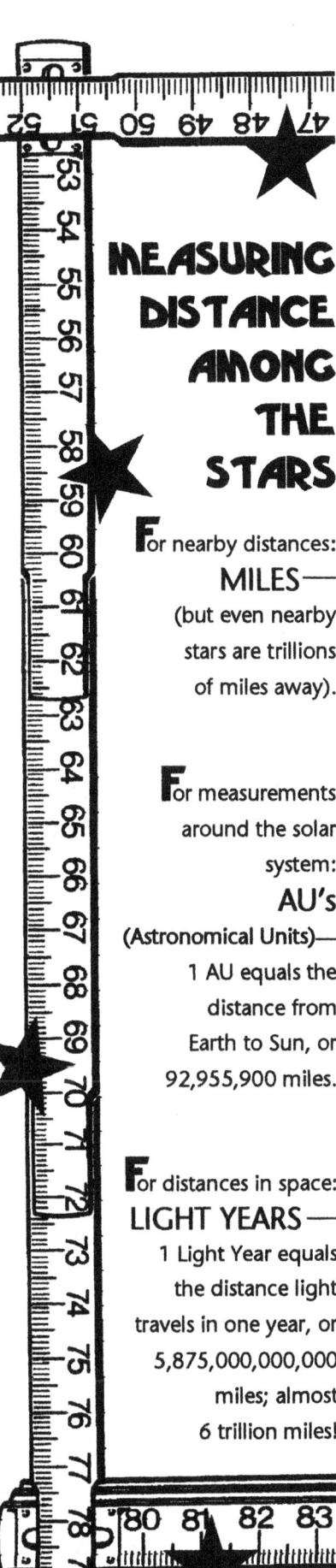

HOW CLOSE ARE... THE NEAREST STARS?

	Light Years
★ Proxima Centauri	—4.22
(or, 270,000 times farther away than the sun)	
★ Alpha Centauri	—4.35
★ Barnard's Star	—5.98
★ Wolf 359	—7.75
★ Lalande 21185	—8.22
★ Luyten 726-8	—8.43
★ Sirius	—8.65

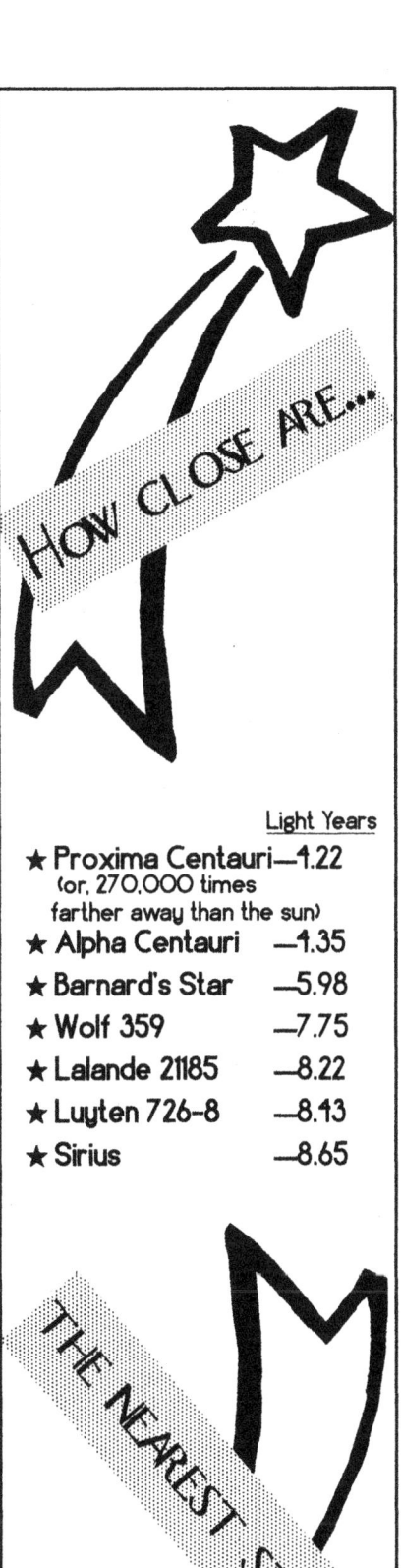

THE MIGHTY TELESCOPE:

- Before 1608, astronomers could only measure what they could see with the naked eye. The greatest single development for astronomy is the telescope.
- First telescope: 1608, by Dutch spectacle maker Hans Lippersky—"The Magnifying Tube."
- First true telescope: 1609, by Galileo.
- First reflecting telescope: 1672, by Isaac Newton.
- World's biggest telescopes: Keck I & Keck II on Mauna Kea volcano on the Island of Hawaii. It is able to distinguish a car's two headlights at 15,500 miles!

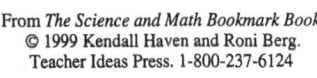

THE MYSTERIOUS MOON:

℘ he same side always faces Earth. You've never seen the back side of the Moon.

℘ he big mystery—where did it come from? No one knows for sure.

℘ he Moon creates our ocean tides.

℘ he Moon is only 240,000 miles away. It's so close, if you shined a flashlight from the Moon, it would only take the light 0.13 seconds to get here.

℘ he Moon circles around the Earth once every 28 days.

From *The Science and Math Bookmark Book*.
© 1999 Kendall Haven and Roni Berg.
Teacher Ideas Press. 1-800-237-6124

Element Facts

Most common elements:

In the universe:
Hydrogen—(90%)

In the atmosphere:
Nitrogen—(78%)

In the earth:
Iron—(36%)

In you:
Oxygen—(35%)

Rarest natural element:
Astatine (At), element 106, only 0.00056 of an ounce exists.

Newest element:
Unununium, element 111, discovered in 1994.

Hardest substance:
Diamond—which is pure carbon, like soot and ash.

C 6	N 7	O 8	F 9
Si 14	P 15	S 16	Cl 17
Ge 32	As 33	Se 34	Br 35
Sn 50	Sb 51	Te 52	I 53
Pb 82	Bi 83	Po 84	At 85

From *The Science and Math Bookmark Book*.
© 1999 Kendall Haven and Roni Berg.
Teacher Ideas Press. 1-800-237-6124

What are ACIDS & BASES?

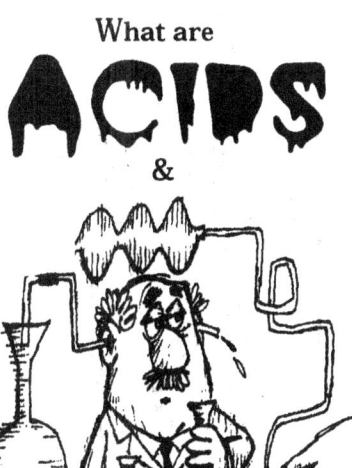

- **Acids** and **Bases** refer to liquids and vapors. Every liquid is either an **acid** or a **base**. There is one exception, *water*, which is neither **acid** nor **base**.

- The titles **"acids"** and **"bases"** group liquids by how they combine with other substances.
    Acids combine by giving up part of each molecule (a proton) to the other substance. **Bases** combine by taking a proton from the other substance.

- **Acids** tend to taste sour and bitter.

- The "strength" of an **acid** or **base** (ph) is a measure of how quickly and fiercely they combine with substances.

From *The Science and Math Bookmark Book*.
© 1999 Kendall Haven and Roni Berg.
Teacher Ideas Press. 1-800-237-6124

What is ph?

We measure the strength of an acid or base on a scale called the ph scale.

Water is neutral and has a ph value of 7.0.

Acids have lower ph values (the lower, the stronger).

Bases have higher ph values (the higher, the stronger).

ph measures the concentration of hydrogen ions (protons) in a liquid substance.

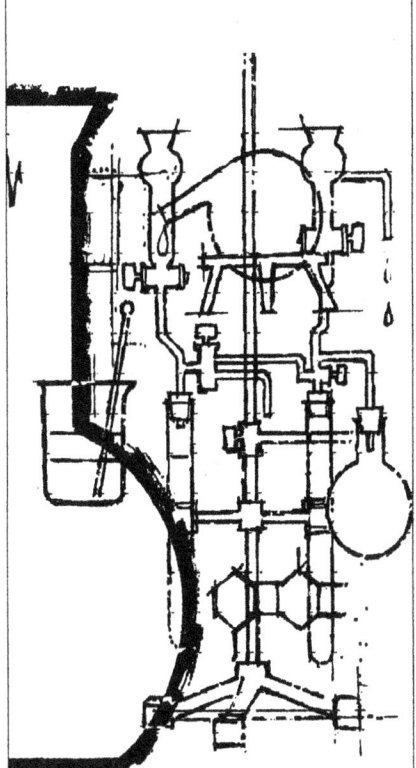

Name some common acids and bases (and their ph strength).

Strongest acid:
hydrofloric acid (HF) mixed with antimony pentafloride—ph 0.001

Battery acid—1.0
Stomach acid—1.5
Lemon juice—2.3
Vinegar—3.0
Coke—3.0
Tomato juice—4.0

Strongest base:
lye—ph 14

Toothpaste—9.5
Dish washing liquid—10
Ammonia—12.0
Bleach—12.9

Carbon (the miracle element)

What is carbon?

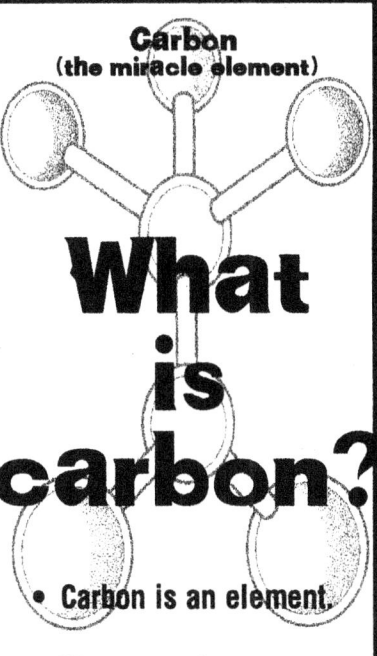

- Carbon is an element.

- We see carbon every day. Ash is carbon, coal is carbon, pencil leads are carbon, diamonds are carbon, black smoke is carbon.

- Gasoline, motor oil, and natrual gas are all carbon-based molecules.

- Carbon is used as the base of over 8 million compounds.

- We exhale CO_2 (carbon dioxide).

- Plants breathe in CO_2.

- We are carbon-based life forms, because the molecules in our bodies are made from chains of carbon atoms.

The Miracle of Salt

We cook with salt, eat salt, require salt to live. It's safe and stable.

It's made of one atom of sodium and one atom of chlorine.

BUT:

Pure sodium (Na) is a soft, corrosive metal that will burn your hand if you dare touch it.

Pure chlorine (Cl) is a deadly, poisonous liquid and gas.

Alone, either could kill you. Put these two killers together and, voila—safe, essential table salt.

What is an Atom and a Molecule?

ATOM: There are just over 100 elements in the world (oxygen, carbon, nitrogen, lead, gold, etc.). Every atom of each element is exactly like every other atom of that element. If you smash an atom of oxygen into its parts (electrons, protons, and neutrons), they no longer act like oxygen, but like electrons, protons, and neutrons.

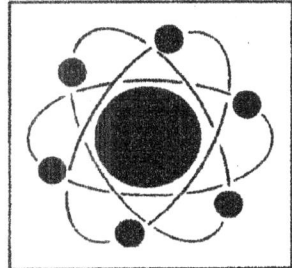

MOLECULE: Every object, every *thing* (mineral, animal, plant, solid, liquid, gas) is made up of molecules. Molecules are collections of atoms fused together. If you break a water molecule into its parts (oxygen and hydrogen atoms), they no longer act like water, but like oxygen and hydrogen.

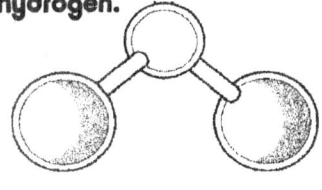

What are some common molecules?

Substances are made of billions of molecules.

Molecules are made up of chains of atoms.

Once joined into a molecule, individual atoms stop acting like their original element and act like part of a molecule of this new substance.

Water: Combine one atom of oxygen and two atoms of hydrogen (both gasses) and you get one molecule of liquid water. We write it as H_2O for two hydrogens and one oxygen.

Salt: Combine one atom of corrosive sodium and one atom of deadly chlorine and you get table salt. We write it as $NaCl$ for one atom of sodium (Na) and one of Chlorine (Cl).

Physical Sciences 14

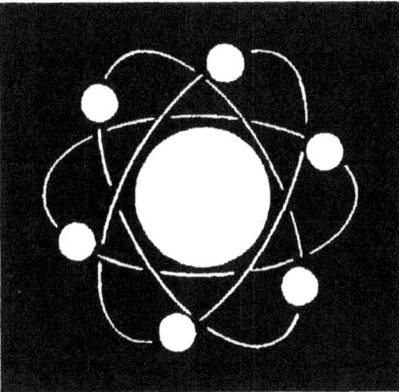

WHAT IS INSIDE AN ATOM?

Two things make up most of an atom:

1. **Nucleus**—is a big ball in the center made of protons and neutrons.

—was discovered in 1911 by Ernest Rutherford of England.

— is like the sun in the middle of our solar system.

2. **Electrons**—are tiny particles that circle in orbits (like shells) around the nucleus.

— circle the nucleus like planets circling the sun.

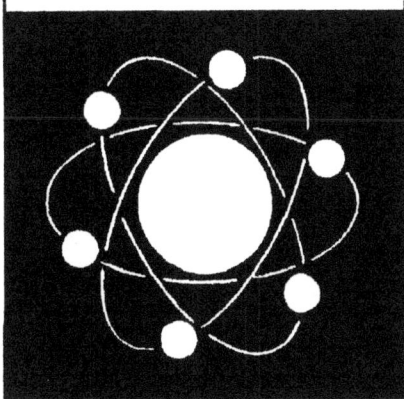

ARE PROTONS AND NEUTRONS THE SMALLEST THINGS INSIDE AN ATOM?

- There are over 200 kinds of tiny-tiny particles that can live in an atom's nucleus.

- All the protons and neutrons in the nucleus are, themselves, made up of smaller particles called "quarks."

- Outside the nucleus, mu- and tau-mesons (like big electrons), and neutrinos (weightless, massless particles) orbit with the electrons.

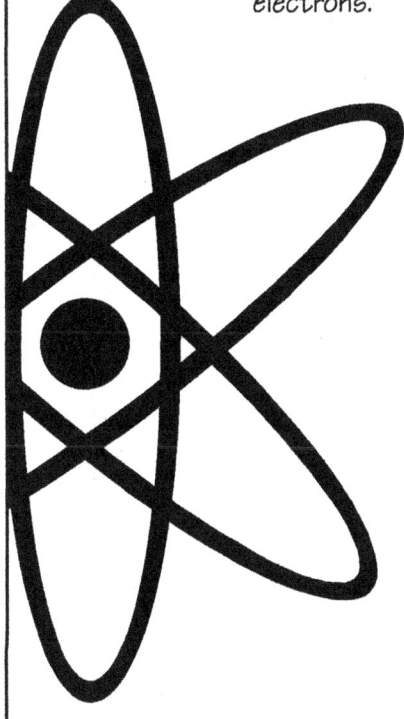

HOW MANY TEMPERATURE SCALES ARE THERE?

Ans: Three

Fahrenheit Scale:
Water freezes at 32°F and boils at 212°.

Centigrade Scale:
Water freezes at 0°C and boils at 100°C.

Kelvin Scale:
0°K = absolute zero, the coldest temperature possible. Even electrons freeze.
0°K = -459.67°F!

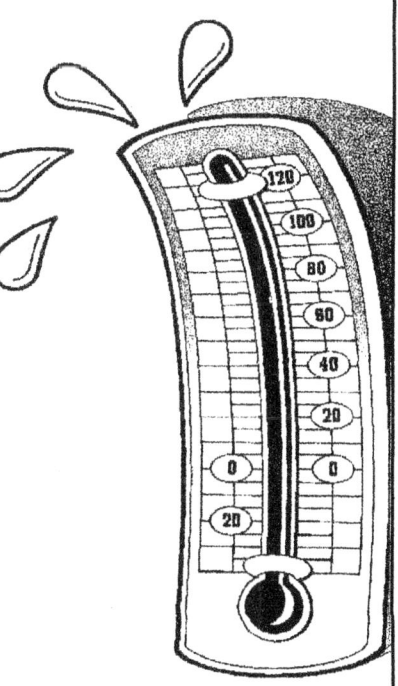

From *The Science and Math Bookmark Book.*
© 1999 Kendall Haven and Roni Berg.
Teacher Ideas Press. 1-800-237-6124

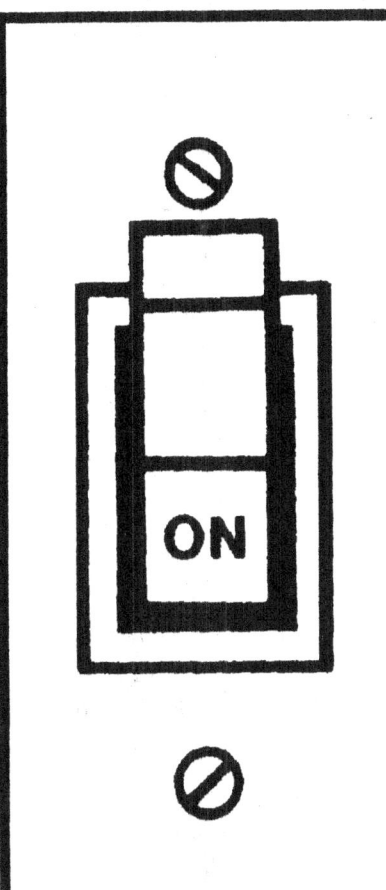

WHAT IS ELECTRICITY?

Electricity is a stream of moving electrons and is called an "electric current."

WHO NAMED THEM POSITIVE AND NEGATIVE?

Benjamin Franklin. (The Greeks called them attractive and repulsive.)

WHERE DO THE ELECTRONS COME FROM?

From inside atoms. Electrons spin around the outside of an atom and get pulled away, or stripped off, to flow as free electrons in an electric current in search of a new atom to live in.

Are there any natural forms of electricity?

Ans: Three.

- **Static Electricity**—Static builds up when you rub one substance against another. It was a popular party game in Colonial America.
- **Lightning**—Deadly electric discharges from violent storm clouds.
- **Chemical Electricity**—Electric eels use chemical reactions to produce electric shocks.

Is there any difference between these three forms of electricity?

Ans: No.
They are all streams of moving electrons.

Great Moments in History:

Ben Franklin's Kite

When: 1750

What he did: Flew a kite into a storm to see if he could collect static electricity from a cloud, just as our feet collect it by shuffling across a carpet.

What he *didn't* do: Tried to attract a lightning bolt. (It would have killed him.)

What he proved: That playful static electricity and deadly lightning were the same, that there was only one form of electricity.

Terms scientists use to

MEASURE ELECTRICITY:

CURRENT: the number of electrons flowing through a wire.

VOLTAGE: the power or potential to do work that each electron carries.

RESISTANCE: Something that impedes the flow of electricity. Common resisters include light bulbs, toasters, and electric ovens. Resistance generates heat.

POWER: a measure of the amount of work done by an electric current. Power is measured in *watts*. The Electric Utility Company charges you by the number of watts you use each hour.

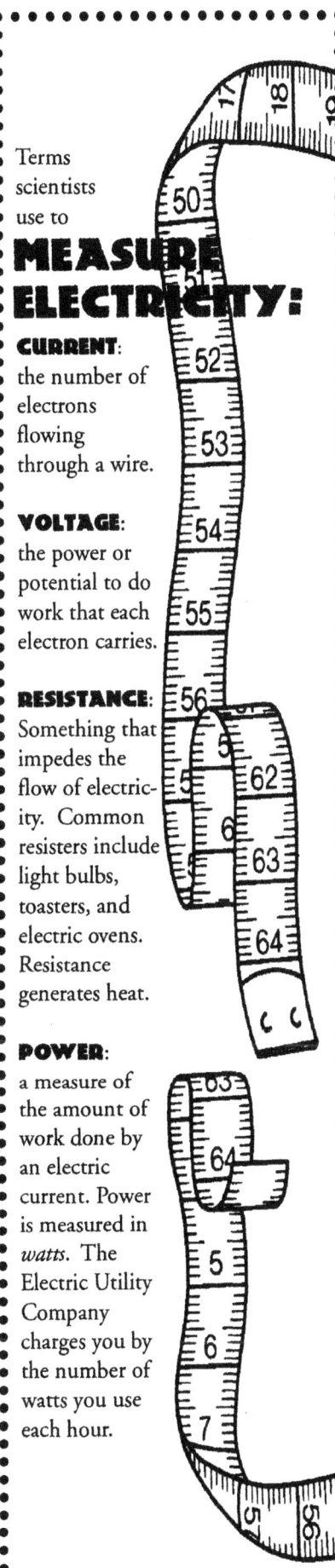

From *The Science and Math Bookmark Book.*
© 1999 Kendall Haven and Roni Berg.
Teacher Ideas Press. 1-800-237-6124

What is artificial electricity?

Ans: Really, all electricity is the same. But, "artificial" electricity refers to electricity produced by humans.

Is it any different from natural electricity?

Ans: No. Electricity is electricity. All flowing electrons are exactly the same.

How can we create electricity?

Ans: Chemical reaction (in batteries) or by using a changing magnetic field (in a power plant).

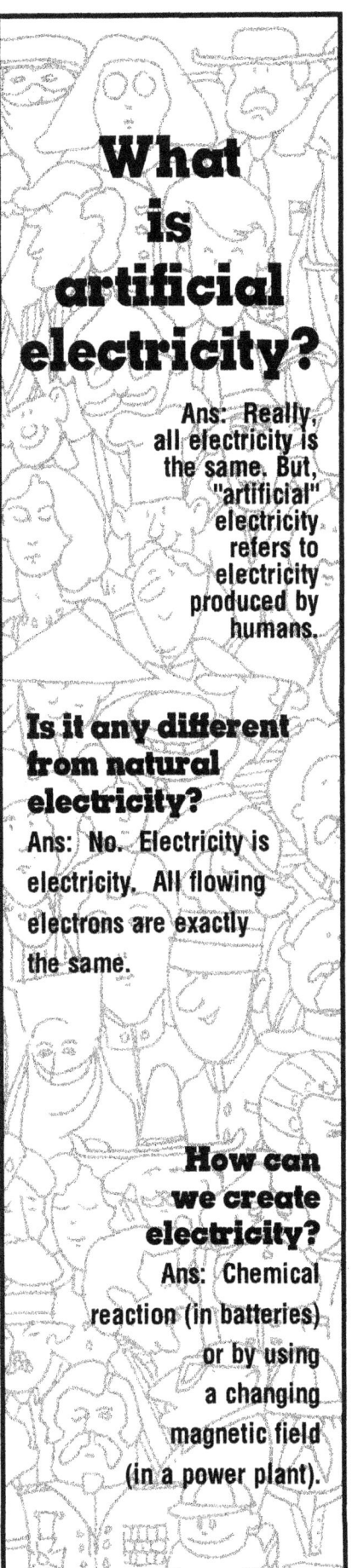

From *The Science and Math Bookmark Book.*
© 1999 Kendall Haven and Roni Berg.
Teacher Ideas Press. 1-800-237-6124

Are electricity and magnetism related?

Yes!

An electric current creates a magnetic field. A changing magnetic field creates an electric current. Magnetism and electric flow are inseparable. They always go hand in hand.

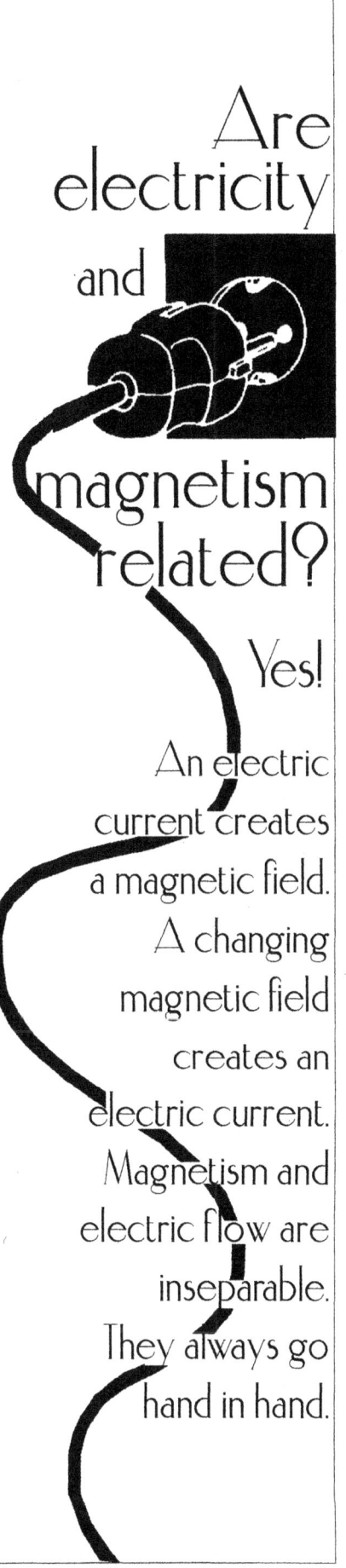

From *The Science and Math Bookmark Book.*
© 1999 Kendall Haven and Roni Berg.
Teacher Ideas Press. 1-800-237-6124

Physical Sciences 17

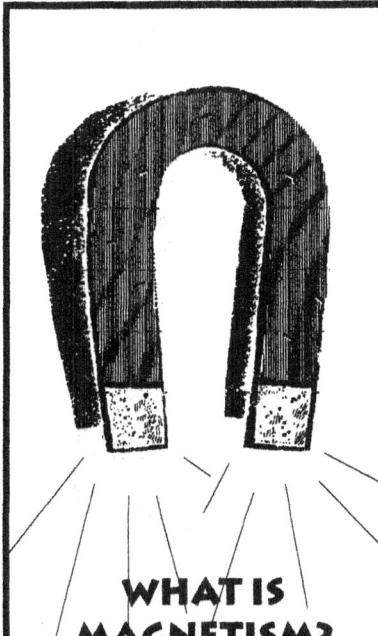

WHAT IS MAGNETISM? WHY DOES THE EARTH HAVE A MAGNETIC FIELD?

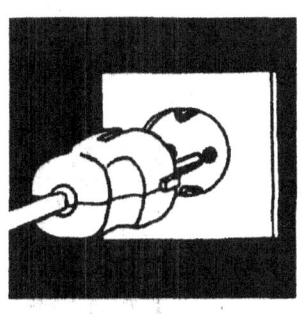

- Magnetism is a basic force of nature.
- Electricity produces it.
- The earth's liquid core circulates, creating an electric flow. That current creates the earth's magnetic field.
- Every electric wire and electric machine creates a magnetic field.
- Magnetism powers your TV, protects the earth, creates the northern lights, makes your compass work, makes motors work, and lets generators create electricity.

From *The Science and Math Bookmark Book*.
© 1999 Kendall Haven and Roni Berg.
Teacher Ideas Press. 1-800-237-6124

What's the difference between nuclear fission and fusion?

- **Fission:** splitting an atom into two smaller atoms. Fission reactions power nuclear bombs and power plants.
- **Fusion:** fusing together two separate atoms into one. Fusion is more powerful, but is still experimental. Fusion powers the stars and the sun.

From *The Science and Math Bookmark Book*.
© 1999 Kendall Haven and Roni Berg.
Teacher Ideas Press. 1-800-237-6124

WHY DOES A LIGHT BULB GLOW?

Thomas Edison is given the credit for inventing the light bulb on Dec 20, 1879, with carbonized cotton filament after 13 years of trying. BUT, Joseph Swan (England) demonstrated his carbon filament bulb on Dec 18, 1878. Edison's design was easier to produce and so overtook the older work and all the credit.

The wire filament in a light bulb is a resistor. It impedes the flow of electricity. The resulting friction gives off heat and light. Because there's no oxygen inside a light bulb, the filament doesn't burn up. It just glows.

From *The Science and Math Bookmark Book*.
© 1999 Kendall Haven and Roni Berg.
Teacher Ideas Press. 1-800-237-6124

Physical Sciences 18

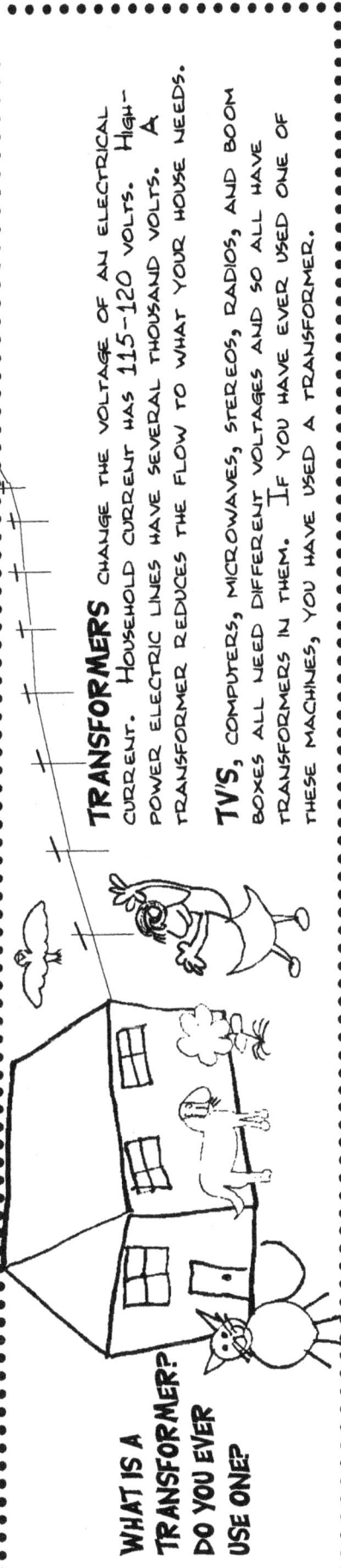

TRANSFORMERS CHANGE THE VOLTAGE OF AN ELECTRICAL CURRENT. HOUSEHOLD CURRENT HAS 115-120 VOLTS. HIGH-POWER ELECTRIC LINES HAVE SEVERAL THOUSAND VOLTS. A TRANSFORMER REDUCES THE FLOW TO WHAT YOUR HOUSE NEEDS.

TV'S, COMPUTERS, MICROWAVES, STEREOS, RADIOS, AND BOOM BOXES ALL NEED DIFFERENT VOLTAGES AND SO ALL HAVE TRANSFORMERS IN THEM. IF YOU HAVE EVER USED ONE OF THESE MACHINES, YOU HAVE USED A TRANSFORMER.

WHAT IS A TRANSFORMER? DO YOU EVER USE ONE?

From *The Science and Math Bookmark Book.*
© 1999 Kendall Haven and Roni Berg.
Teacher Ideas Press. 1-800-237-6124

What is a semi-conductor?

- Some materials (copper, steel, and most metals) are good conductors of electricity. It flows easily through them with little resistance.
- Some materials (rubber, wood, glass) are insulators. Electricity won't flow along them at all.
- A few special materials (like silicone—hence silicon microchips) are sometimes conductors and sometimes insulators, depending on conditions. These are called semi-conductors and are very useful in computers and information storage.

From *The Science and Math Bookmark Book.*
© 1999 Kendall Haven and Roni Berg.
Teacher Ideas Press. 1-800-237-6124

Physics is the study of matter and energy. What is matter? What is energy? How do they relate?

- Matter is all the material that makes up the universe.
- Neither matter nor energy can be destroyed, only changed.
- Matter can change into energy (burning wood, for example).
- Energy can change into matter (photosynthesis in plants, for example).
- Albert Einstein was the first person to discover the true relationship between matter and energy with his famous equation, $E = mc^2$.

See if you can find out what the "E," the "M," and the "C" stand for in that equation.

From *The Science and Math Bookmark Book.*
© 1999 Kendall Haven and Roni Berg.
Teacher Ideas Press. 1-800-237-6124

Ans: They describe the properties of matter:

- Color
- Size (mass or weight)
- Flexibility or Elasticity
- Smoothness or Roughness
- Melting and Boiling Points

- Shape
- Volume
- Density
- Strength
- Rigidity

What other measures can you think of to describe matter?

MEASURING MATTER: How do scientists measure and describe matter?

What's the difference between mass and weight?

MASS measures the amount of matter in an object. Mass never changes.

WEIGHT measures the gravitational attraction of an object to the earth. Weight changes when you change planets.

Important Physics Terms You Will Use:

- **Force:** a push or pull on any object. Forces create motion.
- **Work:** moving a mass through space. Work only happens when there is movement.
- **Inertia:** resistance to change. If an object is at rest, it tends to stay at rest. If it is moving, it tends to continue to move unless acted on by a force. That's inertia.
- **Velocity:** a measure of the speed of movement.
- **Acceleration:** any change in motion in either direction or velocity.

Physical Sciences 20

What is a rainbow?

A rainbow is refracted light, exactly like light refracted through a triangular prism. **T**he sun's light refracts off rain drops in the air. **T**he colors separate as light refracts. **F**or a rainbow to form, the sun must be out and it must be raining. **R**ainbows usually happen in early morning or late afternoon. **I**f you face the sun, the rainbow will be at your back.

From *The Science and Math Bookmark Book.*
© 1999 Kendall Haven and Roni Berg.
Teacher Ideas Press. 1-800-237-6124

What is gravity? Where is gravity?

EVERYTHING exerts a pull on EVERYTHING. We call that pull *gravity*.

Isaac Newton discovered this universal force. As an apple falls to earth, the earth also moves up to the apple. How far each moves is relative to the size of the other object.

The earth is very big. The apple is small. So the apple does almost all of the moving.

From *The Science and Math Bookmark Book.*
© 1999 Kendall Haven and Roni Berg.
Teacher Ideas Press. 1-800-237-6124

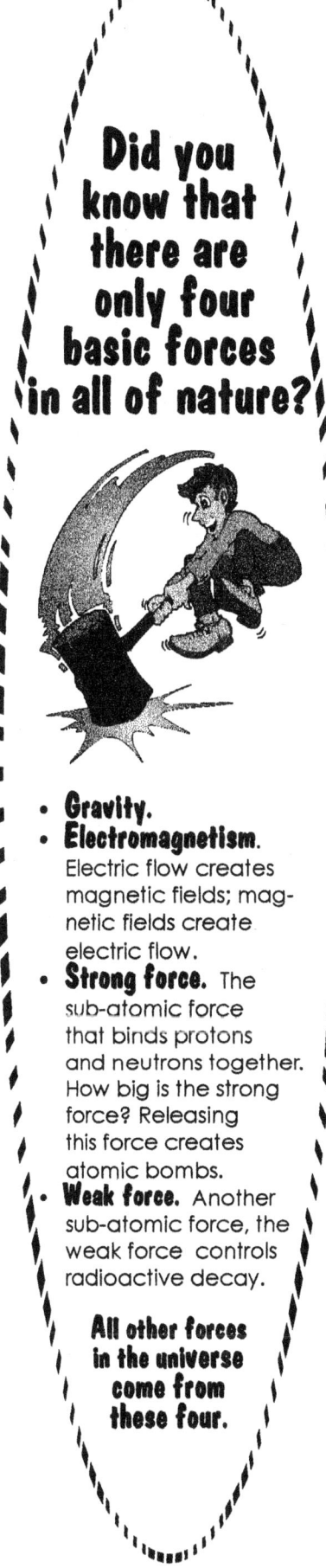

Did you know that there are only four basic forces in all of nature?

- **Gravity.**
- **Electromagnetism.** Electric flow creates magnetic fields; magnetic fields create electric flow.
- **Strong force.** The sub-atomic force that binds protons and neutrons together. How big is the strong force? Releasing this force creates atomic bombs.
- **Weak force.** Another sub-atomic force, the weak force controls radioactive decay.

All other forces in the universe come from these four.

From *The Science and Math Bookmark Book.*
© 1999 Kendall Haven and Roni Berg.
Teacher Ideas Press. 1-800-237-6124

What is friction?

Rub your hands together briskly. The heat you feel is from friction.

- **F**riction is resistance to movement when two surfaces rub against each other. Friction slows motion and produces heat.

- **F**riction was discovered by Count Rumford in 1780 while watching workers bore out cannon barrels in Bavaria.

- **W**hat decreases friction?
  Ans:
  1) sanding and polishing
  2) oils and lubricants
  3) ball bearings

- **W**hen is friction useful?
  Ans: When you want to strike a match, walk across the floor without slipping, drive a car without skidding, keep furniture from sliding and blowing away, tape two things together, use a nail, etc.

How many more uses of friction can you think of?

From *The Science and Math Bookmark Book.*
© 1999 Kendall Haven and Roni Berg.
Teacher Ideas Press. 1-800-237-6124

What is light? What is light made of?

Electro-magnetic waves fill the universe. These are energy waves traveling at every frequency from one wave per second to billions times billions of waves per second.

Our human senses record two specific parts of all those energy waves. We call those two parts *sound* and *light*.

Most parts we can't detect without machines (radio waves, microwaves, X-rays, etc.).

Other creatures record different parts of the spectrum. Many snakes sense infrared, or heat. Dolphins and squids sense ultra high-frequency sonar.

From *The Science and Math Bookmark Book.*
© 1999 Kendall Haven and Roni Berg.
Teacher Ideas Press. 1-800-237-6124

Name the parts of the whole frequency spectrum.

What It Is?	Frequency (Hertz)
Sound	0—30,000
Radio (cell-phones)	10,000—1 million
Radar	1—10 million
Microwaves	10—100 million
TV	1 million—1 billion
Infrared (heat, toaster coils)	10 million—1 billion
Visible Light	1—100 billion
Ultraviolet	100 billion—100 trillion
X-rays	300 billion—100 quintillion
Gamma rays	10 quadrillion—up

Quiz Question: What's a hertz?
Ans: Hertz measures cycles per second for all energy waves.

From *The Science and Math Bookmark Book.*
© 1999 Kendall Haven and Roni Berg.
Teacher Ideas Press. 1-800-237-6124

What is a laser?

Answer:

A laser is nothing more than cooperating beams of light. Most light flies in every direction at a large range of different frequencies, like a crowd milling around a stadium.

In a laser, all light waves have the same frequency, all travel the same direction, and all travel in step with each other, like a marching army of ants. Lasers are powerful and easily controlled because every wave exactly matches every other.

From *The Science and Math Bookmark Book.*
© 1999 Kendall Haven and Roni Berg.
Teacher Ideas Press. 1-800-237-6124

How does a microwave work? How can it heat the soup without heating the bowl?

MICROWAVES ARE HIGH FREQUENCY BEAMS OF ENERGY.

THE MICROWAVE IN YOUR KITCHEN RADIATES BEAMS OF ENERGY AT EXACTLY THE RIGHT FREQUENCY TO MAKE WATER MOLECULES (AND ONLY WATER MOLECULES) FLIP AROUND FASTER AND FASTER. FRICTION HEATS UP THESE WATER MOLECULES AS THEY FLIP FASTER AND FASTER. SINCE ALL FOOD CONTAINS WATER, THE FOOD GETS HOT AS WELL.

THINGS WITH NO WATER CONTENT (LIKE A GLASS BOWL) WILL NOT HEAT UP IN A MICROWAVE.

From *The Science and Math Bookmark Book.*
© 1999 Kendall Haven and Roni Berg.
Teacher Ideas Press. 1-800-237-6124

TIME TRIVIA

Why 24 hours in a day?
Early Egyptians defined an hour as $1/12$ of time between sunrise and sunset. Later, Europeans doubled it to 24 hours to cover the other half of the day.

Why 12 months in a year?
Early civilizations used twenty-eight-day months to match the lunar cycle. They needed 13 months to make a year. Egyptians changed it to 12 months to honor their 12 Gods. They created 12 months of 30 days each plus a five-day end-of-year party—the first New Year's celebration.

Where did leap year come from?

Roman Emperor Julius Caesar was the first who tried to account for the extra $1/4$ day in the year by having a leap year.

From *The Science and Math Bookmark Book.*
© 1999 Kendall Haven and Roni Berg.
Teacher Ideas Press. 1-800-237-6124

TIME TERMS

(Fill in the Blanks)

Millennium=	1,000 years
Century=	100 years
Decade=	10 years
Year=	_____ hours
Month=	_____ hours
Day=	_____ minutes
Hour=	_____ seconds
Minute=	_____ % of a day
Second=	_____ % of a day
Millisecond=	1/1000 sec.
Microsecond=	1/1,000,000 sec.
Nanosecond=	1/1,000,000,000 sec.

How many nanoseconds in a century?
Ans: 31,557,600,000,000,000. That's enough to do most anything!

Can you think of any "time" words not on this list?
Ans: Here are six more: season, week, era, epoch, eternity, moment.

Can you find others?

How small is a nanosecond?
Ans: A nanosecond is to a second what a second is to three years.

From *The Science and Math Bookmark Book*.
© 1999 Kendall Haven and Roni Berg.
Teacher Ideas Press. 1-800-237-6124

WHAT IS RADIOACTIVITY?

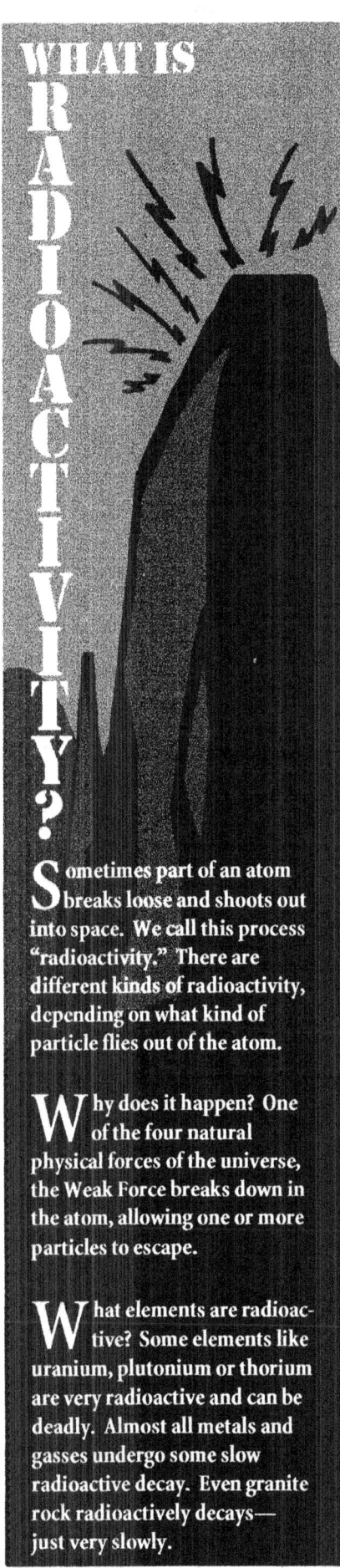

Sometimes part of an atom breaks loose and shoots out into space. We call this process "radioactivity." There are different kinds of radioactivity, depending on what kind of particle flies out of the atom.

Why does it happen? One of the four natural physical forces of the universe, the Weak Force breaks down in the atom, allowing one or more particles to escape.

What elements are radioactive? Some elements like uranium, plutonium or thorium are very radioactive and can be deadly. Almost all metals and gasses undergo some slow radioactive decay. Even granite rock radioactively decays— just very slowly.

From *The Science and Math Bookmark Book*.
© 1999 Kendall Haven and Roni Berg.
Teacher Ideas Press. 1-800-237-6124

Physical Sciences 23

Did you know that there are two kinds of CHEMISTRY?

INORGANIC CHEMISTRY
• Studies the properties of all the elements on the periodic chart.
• Studies the bonds that hold atoms together.

ORGANIC CHEMISTRY
• Is the chemistry of life.
• Studies the carbon and hydrogen chains, which are the basis for all living things.
• DNA is a very long carbon and hydrogen chain molecule with other elements sprinkled in.
• Bones, muscles, brain cells, tree roots, oranges and bread mold—all are made of long carbon and hydrogen chain molecules.
• Many non-living compounds are also made of carbon chains and are studied as part of organic chemistry. Two common ones are: Propane (natural gas): 3 carbon atoms in a chain surrounded by 8 hydrogen atoms (C_3H_8); and sugar (glucose): 6 carbon atoms in a chain surrounded by hydrogen and oxygen atoms ($C_6H_{12}O_6$).

From *The Science and Math Bookmark Book*.
© 1999 Kendall Haven and Roni Berg.
Teacher Ideas Press. 1-800-237-6124

Physical Sciences 24

WHAT IS AN EXPLOSION?

An explosion is a rapid, high-pressure expansion with noise—VERY rapid, VERY high pressure, and VERY noisy.

There are two kinds of explosions:

1. A chemical reaction that happens VERY RAPIDLY and releases heat and light. The generated heat creates expansion, pressure, and noise.
EXAMPLES: dynamite or an atomic bomb. Burning a log could be an explosion if it happened MUCH FASTER.

2. Sudden, rapid release of a pressurized, enclosed gas or liquid.
EXAMPLES: a balloon popping, a tire blowing, a water balloon exploding. Exhaling could be an explosion if it happened MUCH FASTER.

From *The Science and Math Bookmark Book.*
© 1999 Kendall Haven and Roni Berg.
Teacher Ideas Press. 1-800-237-6124

WHAT IS THE SCIENTIFIC METHOD?

The scientific method is a logical way to approach and solve any problem or answer any question. There are five steps in this method:

1. Form a **QUESTION** to answer. (Will a match burn without any oxygen?)
2. Make a guess, or **HYPOTHESIS**, to answer the question. (I think a match *will* burn just as well without any oxygen.)
3. Design an experiment to **TEST** the hypothesis. (Hold a lighted match in a jar that has been filled with helium to drive out all oxygen.)
4. Usually the experiment doesn't work as planned and you must **REVISE** and **RETEST**. (Oops. Helium is lighter than air and didn't stay in the jar. You must invert the jar before filling with helium.)
5. Make a conclusion, or **THESIS**, that summarizes your findings and answers the original question. (A match will not burn without oxygen.)

From *The Science and Math Bookmark Book.*
© 1999 Kendall Haven and Roni Berg.
Teacher Ideas Press. 1-800-237-6124

What makes a rocket move?

A rocket moves for the same reason that a gun recoils when you fire it and a wall holds you up when you lean on it. It is the same principle that makes your chair slide back when you push against your desk.

It's Sir Isaac Newton's Third Law of Motion: for every action there is an equal and opposite reaction.

Gasses shooting out the bottom of a rocket push down on the air and earth. That creates an equal (but opposite in direction) push, or force up on the rocket. If you push against a wall by leaning on it, the wall pushes back on you just as hard. If your feet push on a desk, the desk pushes back just as hard, and that push slides your chair across the floor.

From *The Science and Math Bookmark Book.*
© 1999 Kendall Haven and Roni Berg.
Teacher Ideas Press. 1-800-237-6124

WHAT IS A LIGHT YEAR?

How many light years are there between New York and Los Angeles?

Distances in space are too vast to conveniently measure in miles. Astronomers needed another measure of distance. After Einstein proved that light always travels at the same speed, astronomers realized they could use light as a measure of distance.

A light year is the distance light travels in one year.

It is a very long way! Light travels 186,000 miles in one second and there are 31,577,600 seconds in a year.

A light year equals 5,878,000,000,000 miles, or 5 trillion, 878 billion miles.

It is just over 3,000 miles from New York to Los Angeles. Light could travel back and forth between the two cities 62 times in one second or 2 billion times in one year. 3,000 miles is 1/2,000,000,000th of a light year.

Illuminating news about light

Light is a form of electromagnetic energy, like sound, X-rays, and microwaves. Light lies between infrared and ultraviolet on the electromagnetic frequency spectrum.

Nothing in the universe can travel faster than light.

Light energy travels both as a particle (a photon) and as a wave of energy. Nothing else travels as both.

Light comes in all colors. Its frequency determines its color.

Sunlight contains all the colors and so appears to be white.

Colored light is light with some part of the color spectrum missing.

Light is created when electrons jump inside an atom and emit a photon.

WHAT ARE FLUORESCENT AND LUMINESCENT LIGHT?

- Many materials reflect light. But some substances give off, or emit, light when struck with energy.

- Fluorescent materials emit light only while being struck by energy.

- Fluorescent bulbs and some mineral rocks are examples of fluorescent light.

- Luminescent substances absorb energy and slowly emit light later as they release the energy they have absorbed.

- Glow-in-the-dark watch dials are examples of luminescent light.

What is heat?

Heat is a form of energy. There are two ways we measure heat.

First:

by its potential to do work. This is measured in either calories (metric measure) or British Thermal Units (BTU's). Air conditioners are rated in BTU's to measure how much heat they will pull out of a room. Food is measured in calories as a measure of how much work it could perform in our bodies.

Second:

by the effect of heat. This is measured in temperature. We measure temperature to show how heat has affected the air around us.

Heat can be created by friction, chemical reaction (burning for example), nuclear reaction (the sun for example), or by electrical resistance (an electric heater for example).

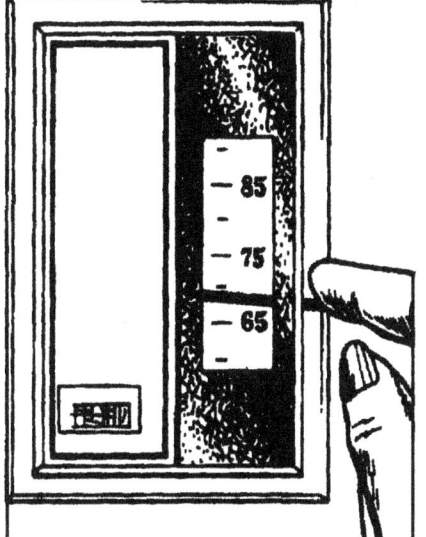

LET'S COMPARE THE TEMPERATURE SCALES

There are three temperature scales: **Centigrade, Fahrenheit, and Kelvin.**

The **Fahrenheit** scale was invented by German physicist Daniel Fahrenheit. One calorie will raise one gram of water one degree Fahrenheit.

One degree on the **Centigrade** scale measures 1/100th of the heat needed to raise water from freezing to boiling.

The **Kelvin** scale was invented by British Lord Kelvin to measure absolute zero. A degree change Kelvin equals a degree change Fahrenheit.

	Centigrade	Fahrenheit	Kelvin
Boiling	100	212	703.69
Freezing	0	32	491.69
Absolute Zero	-273	-459.69	0

To change Fahrenheit into Centigrade:
$C = 5/9 \, (F-32)$
To change Centigrade into Fahrenheit:
$F = 9/5 \, C + 32$

HOT NEWS ABOUT FIRE

Fire is a chemical reaction. It is a form of oxidation. Wood molecules are broken apart and oxygen atoms are added to the free carbon atoms. It is the same process as rust forming on metal, silver tarnishing, or a banana turning brown. They are all forms of oxidation!

Fire requires heat to start the reaction. But once it starts, fire produces heat. It is called exothermic.

Scientists used to believe that heat came from an invisible liquid called caloric. When wood burned, they believed that caloric flowed out of the wood fibers and produced heat. When the caloric had all flowed out, the wood or ashes would no longer feel hot. In 1790, Count Rumford finally proved them wrong and discovered that heat is just a form of energy and that burning creates it.

WHAT IS A VACUUM?

How does a vacuum cleaner work?

Air molecules are all around us. Those molecules push against the things around them, creating pressure. At sea level that pressure equals about 14 pounds per square inch. That's how hard the air pushes on you and every other thing on earth.

If you remove all the air from one spot, there is no pressure there anymore. That is called a vacuum. Remove some of the air and some of the pressure goes away. That is called a partial vacuum.

The fan motor of a vacuum cleaner creates a partial vacuum at the top of the vacuum hose. Air is pushed up the hose to fill that vacuum. As this air rushes into and up the hose, it blows dust and dirt into the cleaner with it.

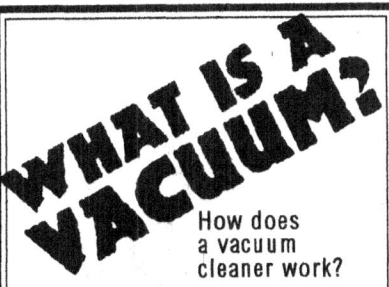

How does a pump work?

A pump is the opposite of a vacuum. A vacuum works by removing gas or liquid and reducing pressure. A pump, such as a gasoline pump, increases the amount of gas or liquid in a fixed space and thus increases pressure.

Spinning blades in a pump push more gas or liquid into a confined space and increase pressure.

What is Pressure?

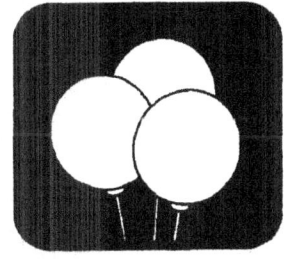

Pressure is the force (or push) one object (or molecule) exerts on another. Muscles can tighten and create pressure. The molecules in a gas or liquid bounce against their container, creating a push or pressure. The more gas or liquid molecules there are in a given space, the greater the pressure.

Force more air into a balloon and it creates more pressure, expanding the balloon until the pressure is too great on the rubber material and the balloon bursts.

That which makes an airplane fly also makes a baseball curve!

Mr. Bernoulli discovered an amazing thing about gasses (like air). The faster gas moves, the less pressure it exerts on the things around it. If one batch of air moves fast and another moves slowly, the slow air will push harder on the things around it.

An airplane wing is flat on the bottom and curved on top. As the plane flies, air has to move faster along the longer curved top of the wing than along the flat bottom. So the air on the bottom pushes harder on the wing than the air on the top and pushes the wing (and plane) up.

As a ball spins and flies, air on one side is forced to move faster because of the spin. Air on that side exerts less pressure than on the other side and the ball curves. Pitchers get strike-outs thanks to Mr. Bernoulli!

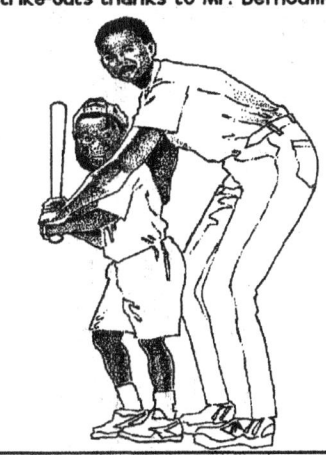

Physical Sciences 28

WHAT'S A COMET?

Comets are left-over bits of ice and dust that didn't form into planets when the solar system began. Their solid cores are made of dust, rock, ice, and frozen gases: carbon dioxide, carbon monoxide, methane, and ammonia.

Comets' long tails are made of streams of dust and gas pulled from the comet by the heat and gravity of the sun as the comet zooms past.

Comets take from 3 years to over 70,000 years to circle the sun.

Can you name some famous comets? Recent visitors near Earth include:

- Hale-Bopp (1996)
- Hyaukutake (1995)
- Haley's Comet (1986)
- Kohoutek (1973)

ASTRONOMY EXPERIMENT

Calculate the angle (azimuth) to a star.

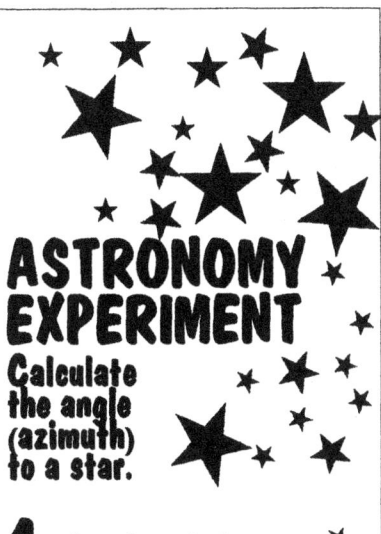

1 Pound a stake into the ground.

2 Find the North Star. Look in the northern sky for the Big Dipper constellation. Look at the two stars that form the front lip of the bowl of the Big Dipper. Follow along a line through those two stars. The first star you find will be the North Star.

3 Lay a rope or wire along the ground from your stake toward the North Star.

4 Stand with your back against your stake and face the star you want to measure. Sight down a pole or ruler toward your star. Lower the ruler to the ground while still pointing it at the star. Lay it between your feet so that one end touches the pole.

5 The angle between the rope and the ruler tells you the angle, or azimuth, to your star. Now you can find it with a compass anytime, anywhere.

---

111 Elements

"Elementary" Information

There are 111 different elements in our world.

93 of them occur naturally in the world.

18 are manmade.

WHAT MAKES AN ELEMENT AN ELEMENT? An element is a substance with a specific number of protons in the nucleus of its atoms. All oxygen atoms, for example, have 8 protons in their nucleus. Most oxygen atoms also have 8 electrons and 8 neutrons. But you can knock an electron or neutron away and it will still act like an atom of oxygen.

If you pulled a proton out of the nucleus of an oxygen atom, the atom would no longer look like and act like oxygen, but like nitrogen, the element with 7 protons in its nucleus.

NAME SOME COMMON ELEMENTS: hydrogen, oxygen, nitrogen, gold, silver, copper, zinc, chlorine, helium, uranium, lead, and sodium are twelve of the 93 naturally occurring elements.

The PERIODIC TABLE of ELEMENTS

For years scientists searched for ways to organize the chemical elements into some meaningful order. As more and more elements were discovered, the problem grew worse.

In 1869, a wild Russian, Dimitri Mendelyeev, realized that chemical elements acted like notes on the piano. Every eighth note is a "C" and has similar characteristics.

Mendelyeev realized chemical elements acted the same way. He organized the lighter elements into rows of eight elements per row, metals on the left, non-metals on the right. By adding extra columns in the lower rows for the heavier transition metals, he found that he had grouped the elements so that the elements in each column all had similar characteristics: melting point, metal or non-metal, tendency to combine with other elements, etc.

The world laughed and called him "the crazy Russian." Within ten years they realized he was right! We still use his Periodic Table of Elements today, over 100 years later.

MIXTURES AND COMPOUNDS

In a **MIXTURE** substances are mixed together but still retain their individual properties. Mix flour and salt in a bowl, and the flour is still flour; the salt is still salt. Ice cream and root beer can be mixed in a glass, but each molecule of ice cream will still be ice cream, even though you can no longer separate them from the root beer molecules.

In a **COMPOUND** substances combine on a molecular level to form a new substance. Combine hydrogen and oxygen and you get water, a whole new substance. Hydrogen and oxygen are no longer present as separate gasses. Now they are a new compound called water.

WHAT'S THE DIFFERENCE?

HOW BIG IS AN ATOM?

Atoms are *tiny!* The smallest and lightest atom is hydrogen with only one proton and one electron. A hydrogen atom is about 0.1 nano-meters across. Over 40 billion could comfortably fit on the head of the sharpest needle. That's 40,000,000,000 atoms in that tiny space! Just imagine how many atoms there are in your body!

The biggest and heaviest naturally occurring atom is Plutonium. It's 250 times heavier than hydrogen, but only three times bigger.

How does a power plant create electricity?

Electricity is created by a changing magnetic field. A changing magnetic field is created by spinning large metal coils in the presence of a magnet.

WHAT SPINS THE COILS?
The metal coils are hooked to the shaft of a giant turbine. As the shaft turns, the magnet turns.

WHAT TURNS THE TURBINE SHAFT?
The other end of the turbine shaft is connected to fan blades. High-pressure steam blows across these blades and spins them, turning the shaft. In hydroelectric plants it's jets of water instead of steam that turn the turbine blades.

WHAT CREATES THE STEAM?
Giant boilers, where either oil, coal, or natural gas is burned, create enough heat to boil a liquid and create steam. In a nuclear power plant, nuclear reactions create the heat. It's smoke from the chimneys of these boilers that blows out pollution from a power plant.

What are the different types of power plants?

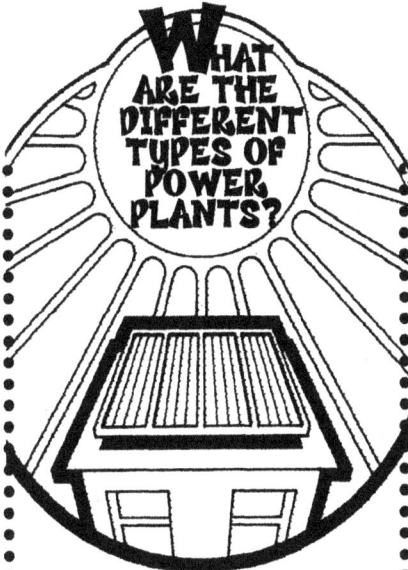

FOSSIL FUEL PLANTS
They burn oil, coal, or natural gas to create electricity. They have tall smoke stacks and huge fuel storage yards next to the plant. These are the most common type of power plant.

HYDROELECTRIC PLANTS (water powered)
Hydroelectric plants are located at dams. The water behind the dam is hundreds of feet deep and creates tremendous pressure. Pipes allow this high-pressure water to escape past turban blades to create electricity.

NUCLEAR PLANTS
It was once thought that nuclear power would provide most of America's energy because each pound of fuel can create so much heat. However, nuclear plants proved too expensive to build, and they create dangerous radioactive waste. No new nuclear plants have been built in almost twenty years.

GEOTHERMAL PLANTS
Geothermal plants use steam that naturally rises from deep in the earth to produce electricity.

OTHER KINDS
Several kinds of renewable energy sources are being used on a small scale. These include municipal trash, solar energy, wind energy, and ocean thermal energy.

How does a telephone work?

1. When you speak, the sound waves of your voice vibrate a rubber diaphragm inside the telephone mouth piece.

2. A small electric current flows through a chamber of carbon grains behind that diaphragm. When your voice pushes the diaphragm in, the carbon is squeezed tighter together and the power of the electric current increases. When the diaphragm vibrates out, the carbon is looser and the current's power decreases.

3. Changes in the amount of power in electric current in the phone line now match the pattern of the sound waves of your voice.

4. The electric current is sent through phone lines to a receiver in the ear piece of a phone that works just like the speakers of a stereo.

IMPORTANT STEPS IN THE DEVELOPMENT OF FLIGHT

THE TIMELINE OF FLIGHT

- 1783—First hot air balloon ascent (by Jean Pilatre)
- 1804—First heavier-than-air glider (by Sir George Cayley)
- 1896—First steam-engine plane flight (by Samuel Langley)
- 1903—First engine-powered, heavier-than-air flights (by the Wright Brothers)
- 1907—First helicopter flight (by Paul Cornu)
- 1909—First flight across large water—the English Channel (by L. Bleriot)
- 1913—First four-engine plane flight (by Igor Sikorsky)
- 1939—First flight of a jet aircraft (by German military)
- 1947—First supersonic flight (by Chuck Yeager)
- 1947—First supersonic plane, the Bell X-1
- 1958—First man-made object to orbit in space (Russian Sputnik)
- 1970—First flight by a jumbo jet (Boeing 747)
- 1976—First flight by a supersonic transport plane (the French Concord)

How much would you weigh on other planets?

How much you weigh depends on the gravitational pull of the planet you stand on. Gravity depends on the size, or mass, and density of the planet. If you weigh 100 pounds on Earth, you'd weigh:

- 38.5 pounds on Mercury
- 88 pounds on Venus
- 9 pounds on the Moon
- 38 pounds on Mars
- 253 pounds on Jupiter
- 107 pounds on Saturn
- 91 pounds on Uranus
- 114 pounds on Neptune
- 7 pounds on Pluto

Car Talk

The word automobile was invented in France in 1890 as a combination of Greek and French words that mean "self moving."

Almost 2/3 of American households own two cars. We drive over 2.4 trillion miles each year, or 14 times to the sun and back.

SOME IMPORTANT AUTO FIRSTS:

- 1770—First steam-powered auto (by Nicolas Cugnot)
- 1801—First 4-wheel auto (by Richard Trevithick)
- 1885—First gasoline engine and first drive shaft (by Carl Benz)
- 1895—First air-filled tires (by Michelin Company)
- 1897—First commercially successful auto, the Stanley Steamer (by the Stanley brothers)
- 1908—First auto assembly line—for Ford Model T (by Henry Ford)
- 1912—First electric starter (by Charles Kettering)
- 1926—Power steering invented (by Francis Davis)
- 1939—First automatic transmission (by General Motors)

Rockets Red Glare...

A rocket is any projectile driven by the rearward expulsion of gasses which are produced by the burning of fuel inside it. A rocket is the only known form of propulsion that works in space.

SOME IMPORTANT ROCKET FIRSTS:

- **1223**—First recorded use of a rocket (in China)
- **1804**—First rocket fired with an explosive warhead (by William Congreve)
- **1812**—First use of a rocket in battle (by the British during the War of 1812)
- **1846**—Fins replace long wooden pole for stability and guidance (by William Hale)
- **1861-5**—First war in which both sides used rockets (American Civil War)
- **1903**—Theory of modern rocketry developed (by Konstantin Tsiolkovsky)
- **1926**—First liquid-fueled rocket (by Robert Goddard)
- **1944**—First intracontinental rocket (the V-2 by German military)
- **1949**—First rocket to reach space (Viking rocket by US Navy)

From *The Science and Math Bookmark Book.*
© 1999 Kendall Haven and Roni Berg.
Teacher Ideas Press. 1-800-237-6124

SOME SIGNIFICANT INVENTIONS BEFORE 1800

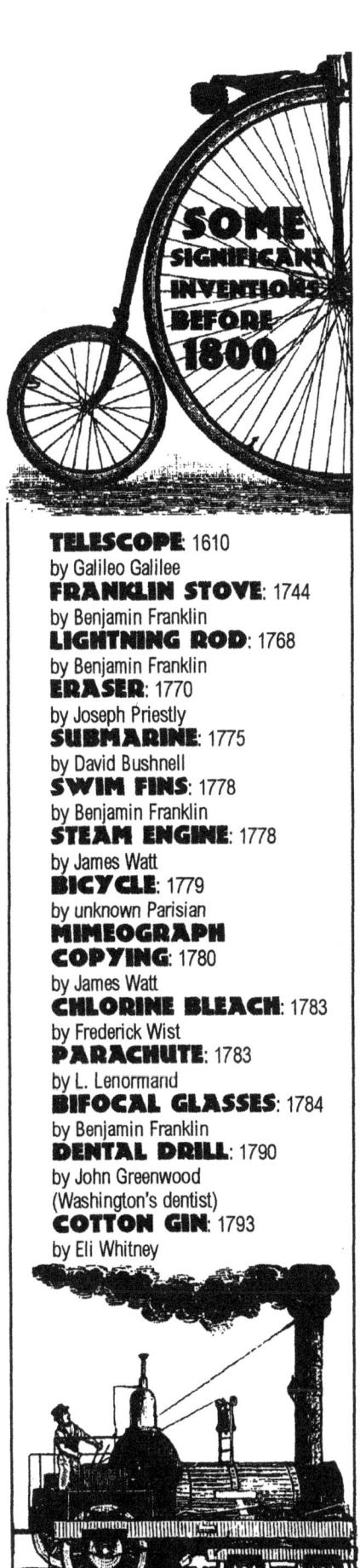

- **TELESCOPE**: 1610 by Galileo Galilee
- **FRANKLIN STOVE**: 1744 by Benjamin Franklin
- **LIGHTNING ROD**: 1768 by Benjamin Franklin
- **ERASER**: 1770 by Joseph Priestly
- **SUBMARINE**: 1775 by David Bushnell
- **SWIM FINS**: 1778 by Benjamin Franklin
- **STEAM ENGINE**: 1778 by James Watt
- **BICYCLE**: 1779 by unknown Parisian
- **MIMEOGRAPH COPYING**: 1780 by James Watt
- **CHLORINE BLEACH**: 1783 by Frederick Wist
- **PARACHUTE**: 1783 by L. Lenormand
- **BIFOCAL GLASSES**: 1784 by Benjamin Franklin
- **DENTAL DRILL**: 1790 by John Greenwood (Washington's dentist)
- **COTTON GIN**: 1793 by Eli Whitney

From *The Science and Math Bookmark Book.*
© 1999 Kendall Haven and Roni Berg.
Teacher Ideas Press. 1-800-237-6124

SOME SIGNIFICANT INVENTIONS BETWEEN 1800 AND 1850

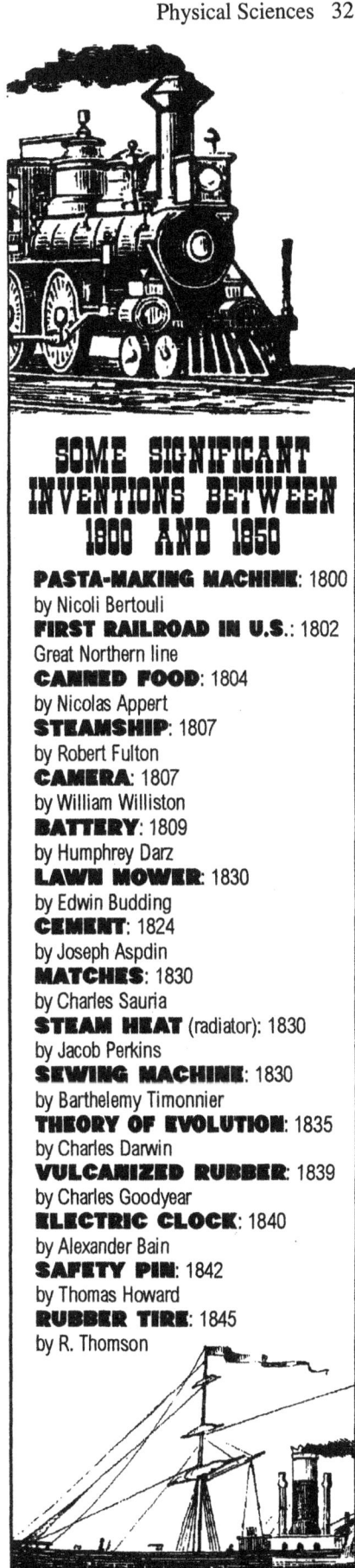

- **PASTA-MAKING MACHINE**: 1800 by Nicoli Bertouli
- **FIRST RAILROAD IN U.S.**: 1802 Great Northern line
- **CANNED FOOD**: 1804 by Nicolas Appert
- **STEAMSHIP**: 1807 by Robert Fulton
- **CAMERA**: 1807 by William Williston
- **BATTERY**: 1809 by Humphrey Darz
- **LAWN MOWER**: 1830 by Edwin Budding
- **CEMENT**: 1824 by Joseph Aspdin
- **MATCHES**: 1830 by Charles Sauria
- **STEAM HEAT** (radiator): 1830 by Jacob Perkins
- **SEWING MACHINE**: 1830 by Barthelemy Timonnier
- **THEORY OF EVOLUTION**: 1835 by Charles Darwin
- **VULCANIZED RUBBER**: 1839 by Charles Goodyear
- **ELECTRIC CLOCK**: 1840 by Alexander Bain
- **SAFETY PIN**: 1842 by Thomas Howard
- **RUBBER TIRE**: 1845 by R. Thomson

From *The Science and Math Bookmark Book.*
© 1999 Kendall Haven and Roni Berg.
Teacher Ideas Press. 1-800-237-6124

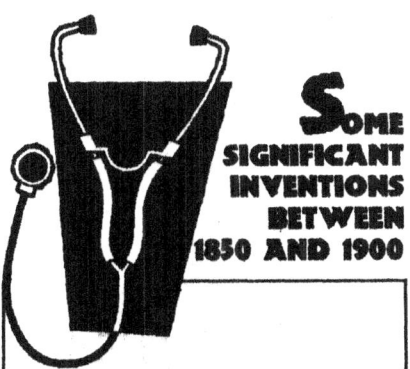

Some Significant Inventions Between 1850 and 1900

STETHOSCOPE: 1850
by C. Cainman
JEANS: 1850
by Levi Strauss
ICE CREAM: 1851
by Jacob Fussell
ELEVATOR: 1858
by Leon Otis
BINOCULARS: 1859
by Jacob Snider
OIL WELL: 1859
by Edward Drake
POSTCARD: 1861
by John Charlton
WASHING MACHINE: 1862
by New York's Hotel Berwick
ROLLER SKATES: 1863
by J. Plimpton
FIRE ALARM: 1873
by Alfred Grechi
MILK CHOCOLATE: 1875
by Daniel Peter
TELEPHONE: 1875
by Alexander Graham Bell
TOMATO KETCHUP: 1877
by Henry Heinz
RECORD PLAYER (phonograph): 1878
by Thomas Edison
LIGHT BULB: 1879
by Thomas Edison
FLUSH TOILET: 1889
by David Bostel
BREAKFAST CEREAL (packaged): 1893
by Henry Perky (shredded wheat)
RADIO: 1895
by Guglielmo Marconi
MOTOR CYCLE: 1895
by Capel Holdren
X-RAYS: 1895
by Wilhelm Rontgen

From *The Science and Math Bookmark Book*.
© 1999 Kendall Haven and Roni Berg.
Teacher Ideas Press. 1-800-237-6124

Some Significant Inventions Between 1900 and 1940

ALKALINE BATTERY: 1900
by Thomas Edison
PAPER CLIP: 1900
by Johann Vasler
AIR CONDITIONING: 1902
by Willis Carrier
MOTORIZED AIRPLANE: 1903
by the Wright Brothers
STAINLESS STEEL: 1912
by Harry Brearley
CROSSWORD PUZZLE:
1913, by Arthur Wyman
TRAFFIC LIGHT: 1914
by Alfred Benesch
ARMORED TANK: 1915
by Walter Wilson
PEANUT BUTTER: 1917
by Washington Carver
ELECTRIC MIXER: 1918
by the Universal Company
HEARING AID: 1923
by Marconi, Ltd.
FROZEN FOOD: 1923
by Clarence Birdseye
TELEVISION: 1927
by Philo Farnsworth
SCOTCH TAPE: 1930
by Richard Drem
CAR RADIO: 1932
by Studebaker
CANDY BAR (Mars bar): 1932
by Francis Mars
NYLON: 1938
by Wallace Carothers
JET AIRCRAFT: 1939
by Heinkel Co.

From *The Science and Math Bookmark Book*.
© 1999 Kendall Haven and Roni Berg.
Teacher Ideas Press. 1-800-237-6124

Some Significant Inventions Between 1940 and 1980

RADAR: 1940
by S. Tucker
TV AD: 1941
by WBNT in New York
SILLY PUTTY®: 1944
by James Wright
COMPUTER: 1944
by Howard Aiken
MICROWAVE OVEN: 1946
by Percy Spencer
TUPPERWARE®: 1946
by Earl Tupper
HOLOGRAPHIC IMAGE: 1947
by Denis Gabor
MCDONALD'S BURGER: 1948
by Richard McDonald
COPIER: 1950
by Xerox
LIQUID PAPER®: 1952
by Bette Nesmith
COLOR TV: 1954
by Alan Walsh
TRANSISTOR RADIO: 1954
by Regency Electronics
CONTACT LENS: 1956
by Norman Bier
VIDEO TAPE: 1956
by Charles Ginsbay
SATELLITE: 1957
USSR (Sputnik I)
POST-IT NOTES®: 1970
Spencer Silver
PAGER: 1971
by Motorola
VIDEO GAMES: 1972
by Nolan Bushnell (Pong)
SKATEBOARD: 1973
by Frank Nasworthy
WORD PROCESSOR: 1978
by An Wang
WALKMAN®: 1979
by Sony Corp.

From *The Science and Math Bookmark Book*.
© 1999 Kendall Haven and Roni Berg.
Teacher Ideas Press. 1-800-237-6124

Physical Sciences 34

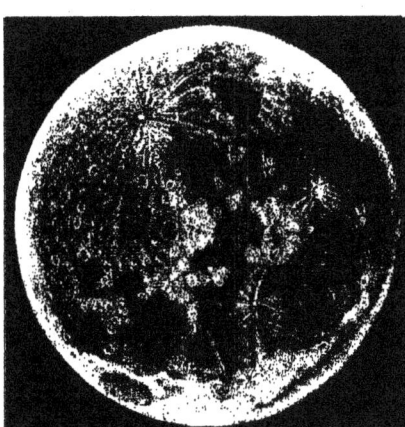

When does a full moon rise?

EVERY FULL MOON RISES AT SUNSET. DO YOU KNOW WHY?

THE LIGHT WE SEE ON THE MOON AT NIGHT IS SUNLIGHT REFLECTED OFF THE MOON. WHEN WE SEE THE WHOLE ROUND MOON, IT MEANS THAT WE SEE THE SAME HALF OF THE MOON THAT THE SUN SEES. THAT ONLY HAPPENS WHEN THE SUN AND MOON ARE ON OPPOSITE SIDES OF THE EARTH. ON THOSE DAYS, THE MOON RISES JUST AS THE SUN SETS.

NEW MOONS HAPPEN WHEN THE MOON AND SUN ARE ON THE SAME SIDE OF THE EARTH. NEW MOONS RISE AT DAWN.

ON THE DAYS BEFORE A FULL MOON, THE MOON RISES LATER AND LATER IN THE AFTERNOON. ON THE DAYS AFTER A NEW MOON, THE MOON RISES LATER AND LATER IN THE MORNING.

From *The Science and Math Bookmark Book.*
© 1999 Kendall Haven and Roni Berg.
Teacher Ideas Press. 1-800-237-6124.

Famous Scientists
NICHOLAS COPERNICUS, ASTRONOMER
Discovered that the Sun is the Center of the Solar System

In the middle ages, the powerful Catholic Church declared that Earth was the center of the Universe. For thousands of years scientists had agreed.

Nicholas Copernicus, born in 1474 in Poland, went to a church university and lived free of charge at the palatial cathedral of his uncle, Bishop Waczenrode. The church supplied all of Copernicus' equipment.

Copernicus measured the position of stars and planets every night for thirty years. He discovered that the church was wrong. The sun, not the Earth, was the center of the universe and that the Earth moved through space.

But Copernicus was so afraid of the church's anger, he refused to release his findings. He even put in his will that they couldn't be released for 25 years after his death. When his discoveries were finally released, the world still refused to believe.

From *The Science and Math Bookmark Book.*
© 1999 Kendall Haven and Roni Berg.
Teacher Ideas Press. 1-800-237-6124.

Famous Scientists
GALILEO GALILEE
Invented the Telescope and Discovered How Objects Really Fall

Galileo was born in 1573 in Italy and was a math professor at the University of Pisa when he was 25. He studied pendulums and discovered that what scientists had believed for 2000 years was wrong: all objects fall at the same speed no matter how big they are. No one believed him. He proved it by dropping a rock and a canon ball off the Leaning Tower of Pisa. Both hit the ground at the same time. *Still* no one believed him for another 50 years!

Galileo also invented the telescope and studied stars no human had ever seen before. He proved that Copernicus was right and that the sun was the center of the solar system. No one believed that, either, until long after Galileo's death.

From *The Science and Math Bookmark Book.*
© 1999 Kendall Haven and Roni Berg.
Teacher Ideas Press. 1-800-237-6124.

Famous Scientists

ROGER BACON, ALCHEMIST
Invented Gun Powder and Eye Glasses

Roger Bacon, born in England in 1214, was a famous alchemy experimenter. What is alchemy? It is an early form of chemistry that tried to combine ordinary ingredients to make them much more than what they were.

Bacon was also a Franciscan monk. Daily he combined chemicals to see what would happen. In 1261 he experimented with saltpeter (an ingredient in many fertilizers). He added ground-up charcoal—nothing happened. He added yellow sulfur powder and stirred—nothing. He put the mix next to the window to add sunlight—nothing. He added fire from a candle. BLAM! His mixture exploded. The table disintegrated. Fire belched out the window. A thunderous roar rumbled across the valley, terrifying the people.

Roger Bacon discovered gun powder. He later invented eye glasses.

Famous Scientists

MARIE CURIE, PHYSICIST
Opened the Door to the Atomic Age

In 1895 scientists discovered a strange property of uranium—what we now know is radioactivity. 28-year-old graduate student Marie Curie decided to search for radioactivity in other metals.

She performed chemical experiments to isolate every known metal in a one-ton dirt and rock sample and see if any were radioactive.

Over three years she discovered two new radioactive elements, polonium and radium, and revolutionized physics by discovering that there were smaller particles inside an atom.

She never knew radioactivity was dangerous. She hung test tubes filled with glowing radium around her tiny lab. Viewers described them as beautiful, magical fairy lights. Really they were deadly radioactivity.

Famous Scientists

JOSEPH PRIESTLY, CHEMIST
Discovered Oxygen

Joseph Priestly was a priest who preferred to play with chemistry than to tend to his congregation.

In 1774 he heated mercury oxide, a red powder. A clear gas bubbled up from this reaction into a glass jar.

But what was this new, unknown gas? Air? Some deadly toxin? How would he find out?

He held a match in the jar. It burned like a torch and frightened Priestly. It wasn't *regular* air!

Then he breathed the gas himself to see if it was dangerous. He felt energized and clear-headed. He breathed in more and felt powerful, as if he could run forever.

Priestly called the gas *pure air*. What he discovered was oxygen, one of the most important elements of our world.

Famous Scientists

CHARLES GOODYEAR, CHEMIST
Invented Vulcanized Rubber

Charles Goodyear lived in Philadelphia and thought he could make rubber clothes for his family. But natural rubber was too gooey and melted in summer. It grew too brittle in winter.

He began experimenting in 1834 by adding different chemicals to rubber. He experimented so much he lost his job. He stunk up the house with burning rubber. The family had to sell most of their furniture to buy food.

Still Goodyear experimented, adding more and different elements to his rubber. After five years his family was fed up! To hide one last experiment from his wife, Goodyear tossed a ball of gooey rubber into the stove's firebox.

And that did it. That rubber worked. Goodyear named it vulcanized rubber in honor of Vulcan, the Roman God of fire.

Famous Scientists

THOMAS EDISON, INVENTOR
Invented the Phonograph and Light Bulb

Thomas Edison was one of America's greatest inventors, and is often called the "Wizard of Menlo Park" because he built his lab in Menlo Park, NJ. Edison attacked every project with a fierce intensity, often working for five or six days straight, never leaving his lab and taking only short cat-naps on a couch.

Edison completed both of his most famous inventions, the phonograph and the electric light bulb, in the fall of 1879. Both were called "miracles that would change the world"...and they did.

Edison also invented several types of batteries and improved the design of telephone, telegraph, and motion picture systems. Many consider Edison's greatest invention to be the design of his lab, itself, the first modern research laboratory in the world.

Famous Scientists

WILHELM ROENTGEN, PHYSICIST
Discovered X-rays

In his basement in Wurzburg, Germany, in 1895, Wilhelm Roentgen began to experiment with something Englishman Edward Crooks invented. Crook found he could amplify an electric signal (make it bigger) by passing it across a vacuum.

Roentgen discovered that mysterious, invisible rays also flew out of this vacuum tube that could pass through wood and cement, and even expose photographic plates that had never seen light. These strange rays even made fluorescent particles glow on his fluorescent screen.

Roentgen held up a lead disc between the vacuum tube and his screen and discovered the rays passed right through his arm and left a perfect picture of his bones on the screen.

He named them X-rays. (In math X stands for unknown.)

Earth Sciences

What are the earth sciences, and what do they study?

Geography: the features on the earth's surface.

Geology: the composition, origin, and history of the earth's surface.

Meteorology: the earth's atmosphere, especially as it relates to making the weather.

Oceanography: the ocean environment.

DO YOU KNOW THE SIX LONGEST RIVERS IN THE WORLD?

	miles
Nile (Africa)	4145
Amazon (S. America)	4007
Yangtze (China)	3915
Mississippi/Missouri (US)	3710*
Yenisey (Eurasia)	3442
Yellow (China)	3395

DO YOU KNOW THE SIX LONGEST IN NORTH AMERICA?

	miles
McKensie (Canada)	2635
Mississippi (US)	2348
Missouri (US)	2315
Yukon (Alaska)	1979
St. Lawrence (Canada)	1945
Rio Grande (US)	1760

*The entire length of the Missouri plus the lower Mississippi from its junction with the Missouri to the Gulf of Mexico.

How high can a waterfall get?

Can you name the world's highest?

Can you find the five highest waterfalls on a map?

	feet
Angel Falls (Venezuela)	3212
Tugela Falls (South Africa)	3110
Utigard (Norway)	2625
Mongefossen (Norway)	2540
Yosemite Falls (California)	2425

Did you know that three of America's five highest waterfalls are in one place? (Ans: In Yosemite Valley, CA)

Which cities in the world get the least rain?

	Inches Per Year
Aswan, Egypt	0.02
Luxor, Egypt	0.03
Arica, Chile	0.04
Ica, Peru	0.09
Antofagasta, Chile	0.19

Which are the driest cities in the US?

Yuma, AZ	2.65
Las Vegas, NV	4.19
Bishop, CA	5.61

What's the driest spot in the world?

Coast of Chile between Ica and Antofagasta—0.004 in. per year (That's one inch of rain every 250 years!)

Which cities in the world get the most rain?

	Inches Per Year
Buenaventura, Colombia	265.5*
Monrovia, Liberia	202.0
Pago Pago, Samoa	196.5
Moulmein, Berma	191.0
Lae, New Guinea	182.9

*265.5 inches equals 22 feet of rain, or almost the height of a 3-story building! That much rain is like getting 2/3 of an inch every day all year long!

Which are the wettest cities in the US?

Quillayute, WA	104.5
Astoria, OR	69.6
Blue Canyon, CA	67.9
Mobile, AL	64.6
Tallahassee, FL	64.6

A GEOGRAPHY QUIZ:

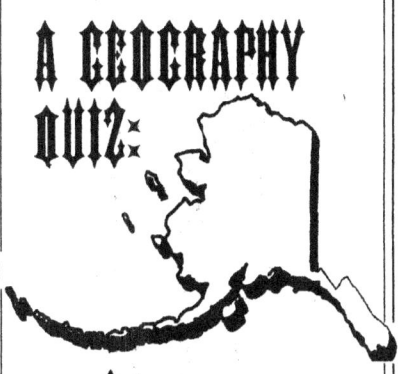

Can you name the northernmost, easternmost, westernmost, and southernmost states in the U.S.?

Answer:
- North: Alaska
- South: Hawaii
- East: Alaska
- West: Alaska

WHY?—

The Aleutian Island chain, part of Alaska, stretches across the International Date Line (the line from which east and west are measured). The last island before the crossing is the westernmost point in the U.S.; the first island after is the easternmost.

What are the northernmost, easternmost, westernmost, and southernmost places in the 48 states that touch each other, called the "Contiguous" 48?

North:
Lake of the Woods, Minnesota

South:
Florida Keys, Florida

East:
West Quoddy Head, Maine

West:
Cape Blanco, Oregon

WHAT IS THE INTERNATIONAL DATE LINE? WHERE IS IT AND WHY DOES IT EXIST?

LOCATION:
North-South between the poles along the line of 180° of longitude (through the western Pacific Ocean) except in the Bering Strait, where it dodges east around the tip of Siberia so that all of Russia is on the same side.

WHAT IT MEANS:
This line marks the place where each day on Earth begins.

WHEN CREATED?:
The Date Line was created in the late eighteenth century when the whole system of longitude and latitude grid lines was laid out at a conference at Greenwich, England.

WHAT CHANGES WHEN YOU CROSS IT?
Two things: The hour changes (as it does when you cross any time zone boundary) and the day changes. (If it's Tuesday on the U.S. side, it's Wednesday on the other side of the line.)

What makes those big underground caverns people tour through?

Answer:
Caverns are created when water dissolves limestone and other mineral-based rocks and then recedes, leaving a hole where rocks used to be. This natural process happens all the time. Most such holes are tiny pits. But when the hole is big enough, it's a cave.

LONGEST:
Mammoth Caves, KY
DEEPEST:
Carlsbad Caverns, NM

Caves are loaded with stalactites and stalagmites.

Which is which and what makes them?

* **"MITES"** stretch up from the floor. **"TITES"** hold tight to the ceiling.

* **Dripping** water rich in minerals makes them both. It drips from the ceiling to the floor, leaving mineral deposits on both that build up like drip candles.

WHAT IS THE YOUNGEST (NEWEST) PLACE ON EARTH?

ilauea lava field on the Island of Hawaii. It's pumping out new land every day as it has been erupting since the mid-1980's. There are places in the Kilauea area where everything you can see—rock, bush, grass, and tree—are all younger than you are!

econd place goes to Surtsey Island, a small volcanic island off Iceland created by a 1963 volcanic eruption.

HOW LOW CAN YOU GO? ARE THERE ANY PLACES ON EARTH THAT LIE BELOW SEA LEVEL?

The seven lowest places on earth are:

	(feet below sea level)
Dead Sea (Israel)	1312
Turfan Depression (China)	505
Qattara Depression (Egypt)	436
Poluostrov (Kazakhstan)	433
Danakil (Ethiopia)	383
Death Valley (California)	282
Salton Sea (California)	235

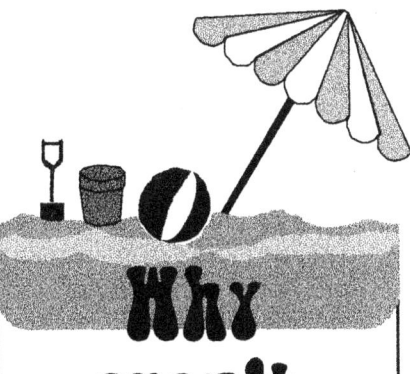

Why aren't places below sea level flooded with water from the ocean?

Answer:
They don't fill with water because they are all in dry areas, far removed from the ocean.

BUT one has flooded. Do you know which one?

Answer:
The Salton Sea. There was no sea in south-central California until a pipe broke in 1911 that had been built to carry Colorado River water to Los Angeles.

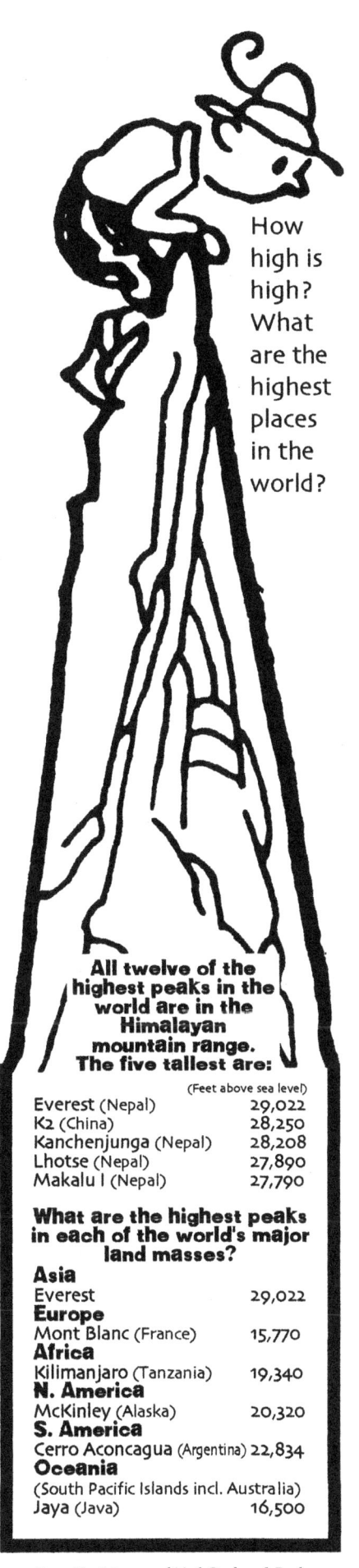

How high is high? What are the highest places in the world?

All twelve of the highest peaks in the world are in the Himalayan mountain range. The five tallest are:

(Feet above sea level)
Everest (Nepal)	29,022
K2 (China)	28,250
Kanchenjunga (Nepal)	28,208
Lhotse (Nepal)	27,890
Makalu I (Nepal)	27,790

What are the highest peaks in each of the world's major land masses?

Asia
Everest 29,022
Europe
Mont Blanc (France) 15,770
Africa
Kilimanjaro (Tanzania) 19,340
N. America
McKinley (Alaska) 20,320
S. America
Cerro Aconcagua (Argentina) 22,834
Oceania
(South Pacific Islands incl. Australia)
Jaya (Java) 16,500

What are the tallest peaks in the U.S.?

ALL TEN OF THE TALLEST U.S. PEAKS ARE IN ALASKA.

The three tallest are:

(Feet above sea level)
MCKINLEY 20,320
ST. ELIAS 18,008
FORALER 17,400

CALIFORNIA, COLORADO AND WASHINGTON ARE THE ONLY OTHER STATES WITH PEAKS OVER 14,000 FEET. (AT 14,494 MT. WHITNEY IN CALIFORNIA IS TALLEST.)

CAN YOU FIND THE OTHER PEAKS ABOVE 14,000 FEET ON A MAP? (HINT: LOOK AT THE MAJOR MOUNTAIN RANGES IN THOSE STATES.)

NAME THE NINE MAJOR MOUNTAIN RANGES IN THE U.S.

Cascade, Sierra, Rockies, Appalachians, Ozarks, Tetons, Catskills, Brooks, and Alaska.

CAN YOU FIND THEM ALL ON THIS MAP?

HOW MANY MORE MOUNTAIN RANGES CAN YOU FIND? ARE THERE ANY NEAR WHERE YOU LIVE?

Ans:
Andes—South America
Himalayan—India, Nepal & China
Urals—Russia
Alps—Western Europe
Sierra Madre—Mexico
Atlas—North Africa
Pyrenes—Spain
Carpathian—Eastern Europe
Great Dividing Range—Australia

CONNECT EACH OF THESE WORLD MOUNTAIN RANGES WITH THE COUNTRY OR CONTINENT IT IS IN:

Andes	Russia
Himalayan	Mexico
Urals	India, Nepal & China
Alps	Western Europe
Sierra Madre	Spain
Atlas	North Africa
Pyrenes	Australia
Carpathian	South America
Great Dividing Range	Eastern Europe

Name the BIGGEST islands in the world:

	(Square Mile Area)
Greenland	2,175,590
New Guinea	789,900
Borneo	751,000
Madagascar	578,041
Baffin Island	507,451

And the BIGGEST U.S. Islands:

	(Square Mile Area)
Hawaii	4037
Kodiak (Alaska)	3672
Puerto Rico (Caribbean Sea)	3459
Prince of Wales (Alaska)	2587
Chicagof (Alaska)	2085

How Big Are The Oceans? Are Oceans Always Bigger Than Seas?

OCEANS:
(Square Miles)

Pacific	63,800,000
Atlantic	31,830,000
Indian	28,360,000
Arctic	5,400,000

SEAS:

Philippine Sea	3,042,000
South China	2,131,000
Arabian	1,492,000
Caribbean	1,063,000
Mediterranean	967,000
Bering	876,000

What's hot; what's not

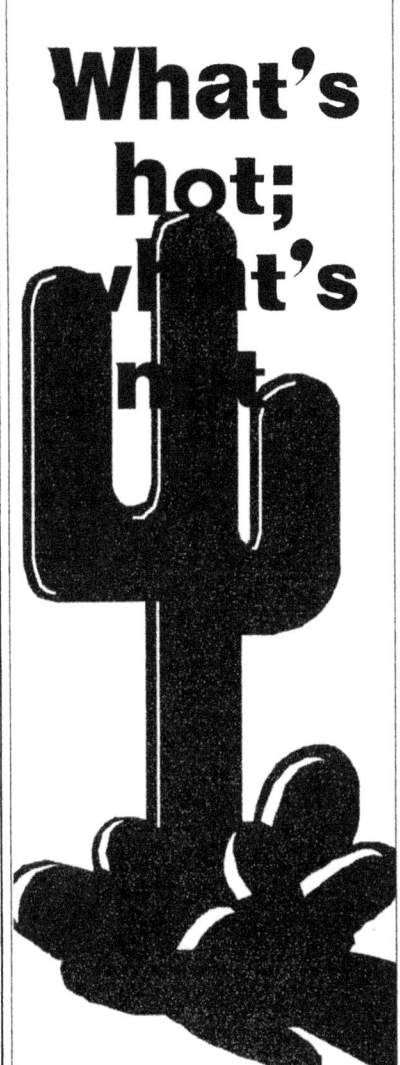

- **Hottest** U.S. spot?
  Death Valley:
  134° F max. recorded
  120° F frequently reached

- **Coldest** U.S. spot?
  Prospect Creek, AK:
  -80° F min. recorded
  -30° F frequently reached

- **Why** are the cold places cold?
  Ans.: high latitude, high altitude, and long distance from an ocean.

- **Why** are the hot places hot?
  Ans.: low latitude, low altitude, and proximity to a warm ocean current.

NAME THE COLDEST & HOTTEST CITIES IN THE U.S.

(THIS LIST DOESN'T INCLUDE ALASKA AND HAWAII, WHICH WOULD DOMINATE BOTH CATEGORIES.)

COLDEST	RANK
International Falls, MN	1
Duluth, MN	2
Caribou, ME	3
Marquette, MI	4
Sault Ste. Marie, MI	5
Fargo, ND	6
Williston, ND	7
Alamosa, CO	8

HOTTEST	RANK
Key West, FL	1
Miami, FL	2
West Palm Beach, FL	3
Ft. Myers, FL	4
Yuma, AZ	5
Brownsville, TX	6
Orlando, FL	7
Vero Beach, FL	8

How many kinds of natural disasters can you name?

Weather Related:
- Hurricane
- Cyclone
- Tornado
- Dust Storm
- Flood
- Drought
- Sand Storm
- Ice Storm

Earth Related:
- Earthquake
- Tsunami
- Avalanche
- Volcano
- Forest Fire

Which ones happen where you live? Which don't?

What are the Tropic of Cancer & Tropic of Capricorn? What do they signify?

Can you find them in an atlas?

Answer:

They are two lines of latitude, 23.5° north of the equator and 23.5° south. The *Tropic of Cancer* is north, the *Tropic of Capricorn* is south.

As the earth circles the sun, the sun appears to drift farther north (in our summer) and farther south (in our winter). The two tropics mark the northernmost and southernmost extent of the sun's drift.

The area between these two lines is called the tropics.

Which U.S. states are in the tropics? **Only Hawaii.**

ABOUT GLACIERS:

- Glaciers are rivers of ice.
- Glaciers hold 5% of the earth's water.
- Biggest glacial sheets are in Antarctica and Greenland.
- Longest: Lambert Glacier (Antarctica) 440 miles long, 40 miles wide.

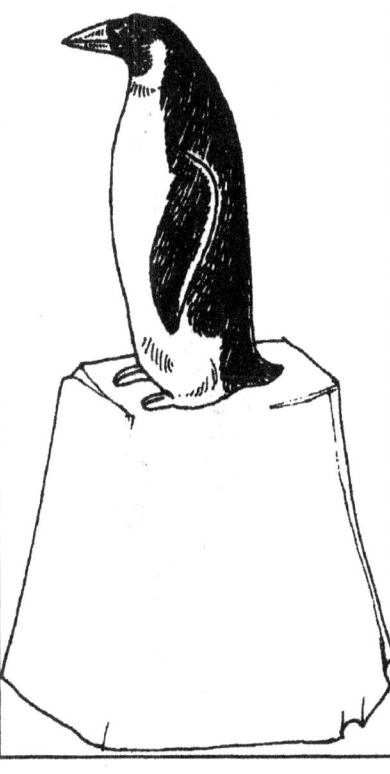

GLACIERS DURING THE ICE AGES

During ice ages, vast glacial sheets extended as far south as northern Illinois. So much water was held in glaciers that sea level was almost 800 feet lower than it is today. The east coast shoreline lay 150 miles farther east (out into the ocean) than it does today.

When glaciers travel through a valley and recede, they leave "U" shaped valleys (instead of rivers, which gouge "V" shaped valleys). In the U.S. there are only two such valleys—Yosemite and Hetch Hetchy, both in California's Sierra Nevada mountains.

WHAT'S INSIDE THE EARTH?

- A thin CRUST about 30 miles thick made of light rock.

- A thick MANTLE about 1800 miles thick of solid, heavy rock.

- A liquid CORE about 1300 miles thick of molten rock.

- A SOLID CORE, about an 800 mile radius, made of nickel and iron.

- It gets hotter as you travel down because the pressure builds and because of radioactively created heat.

ROCK FACTS:

There are three kinds of rocks: sedimentary, metamorphic, and igneous.

The oldest known rock is 3.9 billion years old! It's a small grain of zircon found in Yellowknife, Canada.

The oldest rock formation is 3.8 billion years old in Greenland. (The earth is 4.6 billion years old.)

Where do rocks go when they die? They turn into sand, silt, and dirt.

Earth Sciences 47

Where do the different types of rocks come from?

Igneous— "fire-formed" from cooling molten magma from volcanoes—granite, pumice, obsidian.

Sedimentary— compacted sediments at the bottom of oceans—sandstone, limestone, shale.

Metamorphic— rocks changed from their original form by chemical action, pressure, and/or temperature—marble starts out as limestone, diamonds start as coal.

From *The Science and Math Bookmark Book*.
© 1999 Kendall Haven and Roni Berg.
Teacher Ideas Press. 1-800-237-6124

What is a mineral?

A mineral is any inorganic solid with fixed atomic composition and ordered structure.

There are more than 3,000 known minerals.

Minerals are the base components of rocks.

Many minerals form into crystal.

Some minerals are essential trace nutrients in food—salt is a mineral. Many form precious gemstones.

From *The Science and Math Bookmark Book*.
© 1999 Kendall Haven and Roni Berg.
Teacher Ideas Press. 1-800-237-6124

How do we measure geologic time?

Geologic time spans billions of years. Time is divided into Eras; each Era into Periods; each Period into Epochs.

There have been four eras:
1) Eozoic (more than 345 million years ago)
2) Paleozoic (230-325 million years ago)
3) Mesozoic (65-230 million years ago)
4) Cenozoic (65 million years ago to the present)

Which Era did the dinosaurs live in? (Ans: Mesozoic)

What are the three Periods of this Era? (Ans: Triassic, Jurassic, Cretaceous)

From *The Science and Math Bookmark Book*.
© 1999 Kendall Haven and Roni Berg.
Teacher Ideas Press. 1-800-237-6124

Earth Sciences 48

How do geologists know how old an ancient rock is?

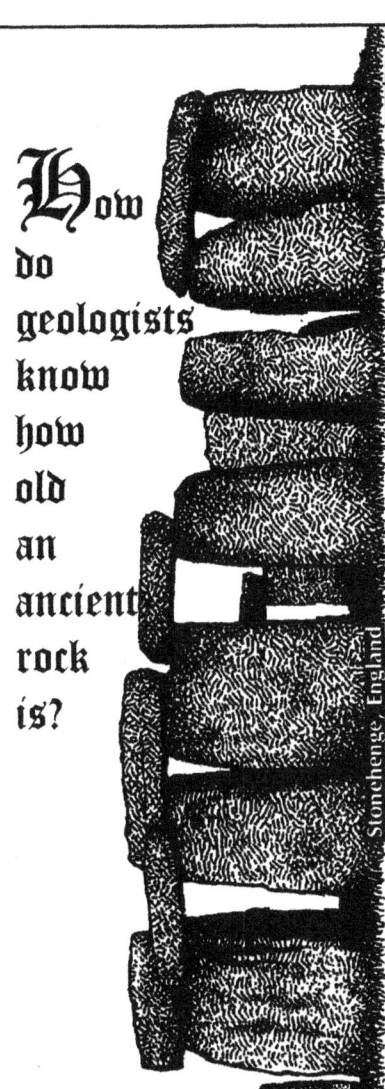
Stonehenge, England

Until this century they could only guess by assuming that the deeper the rock is buried, the older it is.

Then Arthur Holmes made a discovery. He found that one form of carbon (called carbon 14) breaks down very slowly, the way uranium does. He could measure the amount of C-14 left in a rock and tell exactly how old it was.
— The process is called "carbon dating."
— Now other elements, such as argon and potassium, are also used.

From *The Science and Math Bookmark Book*.
© 1999 Kendall Haven and Roni Berg.
Teacher Ideas Press. 1-800-237-6124

Where did atmosphere come from?

The earth was born without an atmosphere.

The atmosphere came from gasses given off by early volcanic eruptions.

The atmosphere is now several hundred miles high, although very little of it is more than 5 miles up.

From *The Science and Math Bookmark Book*.
© 1999 Kendall Haven and Roni Berg.
Teacher Ideas Press. 1-800-237-6124

What Are The Layers In The Atmosphere?

There are three:

1) **Troposphere:** the first 35,000 feet up from sea level.

2) **Stratosphere:** a much thinner layer about 20 miles thick.

3) **Ionosphere:** a loose collection of gas molecules about 150 miles thick.

Only in the bottom half of the Troposphere is there enough air for you to breathe.

From *The Science and Math Bookmark Book*.
© 1999 Kendall Haven and Roni Berg.
Teacher Ideas Press. 1-800-237-6124

Earth Sciences 49

What is a Cloud?

All clouds are really water vapor.

Air always holds water. The hotter it is, the more it can hold. Clouds happen when air rises and cools, losing its ability to hold water. Air cools as it rises and can hold less water. Water condenses into tiny droplets that make up a cloud, just as water condenses onto the side of a cold glass.

Clouds have less water than you'd think. White, puffy summer clouds several miles across may only have 20-30 gallons of water, barely enough to fill a bathtub.

From *The Science and Math Bookmark Book*.
© 1999 Kendall Haven and Roni Berg.
Teacher Ideas Press. 1-800-237-6124

Name the Clouds:

CUMULUS—
Latin for heaped or piled up—big, puffy clouds.

STRATUS—
Latin for stretched out—sheets of clouds that cover the sky.

CIRUS—
Latin for fibrous—high, wispy—often all ice (because of altitude).

Types of clouds:

HIGH, THIN—
cirus, cirrocumulus.

LOW—
stratus, stratocumulus, fair weather cumulus.

MID-LEVEL—
alto cumulus, alto stratus.

STORM—
nimbostratus, cumulonimbus (thunderheads which can be ten miles tall).

From *The Science and Math Bookmark Book*.
© 1999 Kendall Haven and Roni Berg.
Teacher Ideas Press. 1-800-237-6124

How much does air weigh?

The Italian scientist Torricelli first discovered that air had weight in 1532.

But how much does it weigh? All the air above one square inch from sea level to the top of the atmosphere weighs 14.9 pounds.

Does air always weigh 14.9 pounds? No. It changes slightly as high and low pressure weather systems blow through. It also decreases as you climb higher into the mountains.

Why don't you feel it? Because it's always been there, every moment of your life, and really changes very little.

From *The Science and Math Bookmark Book*.
© 1999 Kendall Haven and Roni Berg.
Teacher Ideas Press. 1-800-237-6124

WHAT IS HUMIDITY? WHAT IS DEW POINT?

- Air can hold a certain amount of water in suspension. You can't see it. But it's there. As the air's temperature rises, it can hold more water. As it drops, it can hold less water.
- Humidity is a measure of how much water the air is holding.
- The air right next to a cold drink glass cools and loses its ability to hold water. Water precipitates out of the air as it drops down the side of the glass.
- The Dew Point is that temperature at which the air could just barely hold the water it currently holds. It's called a dew point, because that's the temperature when dew starts to form on grass and leaves.

What's in Air?

ANSWER:
(Most abundant element listed first)

Nitrogen

Oxygen

Water Vapor

Carbon
(CO_2—carbon dioxide,
CO—carbon monoxide,
and maybe soot and smoke)

Sulfur

Rare Gasses

Trace Elements

What is lightning?

In severe storm clouds with strong tumbling internal winds, electrons are ripped from water atoms and bunched. The cloud forms charged layers like a layer cake.

The bottom of a cloud is negatively charged. It actually repels (pushes away) electrons in the ground below, creating a positively charged ground area which runs up trees and buildings, and you, if you stand underneath the cloud.

When the charge builds up big enough, it changes the air under the cloud into "ionized" air. Ionized air is a good conductor. The negatively charged electrons race down the ionized air to the positively charged ground. That's a lightning bolt.

Earth Sciences 51

What is thunder?

Air is super-heated by a lightning bolt. As it heats, it expands and spreads away from the lightning path. After the lightning ends, the air cools and rushes back in from all sides like water after a stone dropped into a pool. Air smacks together, causing the sound wave we call thunder.

From *The Science and Math Bookmark Book.*
© 1999 Kendall Haven and Roni Berg.
Teacher Ideas Press. 1-800-237-6124

Why is the sky blue during the day, red at sunset, and black at night, when air really isn't any color at all?

- The sun radiates light with all colors of the rainbow. But the atmosphere bends light.
- Longer wave lengths (reds and yellows) are bent more than short wave lengths (blues).
- During the day what we see are the remaining blue portions of the sun's light after reds and yellows are bent away from the earth.
- At sunset (and sunrise) we see the red-yellow portions that are bent around the Earth's curved surface.
- At night no sun light reaches us, so the sky is black.

From *The Science and Math Bookmark Book.*
© 1999 Kendall Haven and Roni Berg.
Teacher Ideas Press. 1-800-237-6124

NAME THE SNOWIEST U.S. CITIES

	Inches Per Year
Blue Canyon, CA	240.8
Marquette, MI	128.6
Sault Ste. Marie, MI	116.7
Syracuse, NY	111.6
Caribou, MN	110.4
Mt. Shasta, CA	104.9
Lander, WY	102.5
Flagstaff, AZ	99.9
Sexton Summit, OR	97.8
Muskegon, MI	97.0

BONUS QUESTION: Name the southernmost place in the U.S. that gets snow every year.
ANSWER: Mona Kea, an extinct volcano on the Island of Hawaii, gets 20-30 inches of snow a year and has ski slopes!

From *The Science and Math Bookmark Book.*
© 1999 Kendall Haven and Roni Berg.
Teacher Ideas Press. 1-800-237-6124

What is Fog?

Why does it happen?

Fog is a cloud that forms right next to the ground.

Fog forms when warm air is trapped against the ground, usually in valleys or along the coast. As the air cools overnight, it forms a cloud. But we call it fog because the cloud is trapped against the ground until the sun warms the air so it can reabsorb the water the next morning.

What is wind?

What makes the wind?

Wind is moving air.

Three forces create wind:

Temperature:
Colder (heavier) air over the poles continuously flows toward the equator.

Rotation:
The spinning of the Earth creates steady winds around the globe.

Weather:
Air in high pressure cells always flows toward low pressure cells.

Name the Windiest Cities in the U.S.

MPH AVE.*

Blue Hills, MA	15.4
Dodge City, KS	14.0
Amarillo, TX	13.5
Rochester, MN	13.1
Cheyenne, WY	12.9
Casper, WY	12.9

*average wind speed all day, all night, all year long!!

What's the difference between a SEA and an OCEAN?

- Seas are smaller bodies of water than oceans.
- There are **FOUR** oceans. Can you name them?
  Ans: Pacific, Atlantic, Indian, and Antartic.
- There are over **FIFTY** seas. Sometimes oceans contain seas. (The Sargasso Sea is a region of the mid Atlantic.) Sometimes Seas are surrounded by land (Black Sea, Caspian Sea). Sometimes Seas are partially landlocked (the North Sea and Baltic Sea).
- Ancient peoples tended to name bodies of salt water seas. Ocean is a more modern term, only 500 or 600 years old.

She Sells Sea Shells By The Sea Shore

Here are the names of 21 of the biggest seas:

Black Sea	Caspian Sea
Philippine Sea	Dead Sea
South China	Arabian Sea
Caribbean Sea	Red Sea
Bering Sea	Tasman Sea
Sea of Galilee	Yellow Sea
Adriatic Sea	Coral Sea
Aegean Sea	Sea of Japan
South China Sea	Baltic Sea
Caribbean Sea	North Sea
Mediterranean Sea	

Can you find all of these on a world map? How many more can you find? Hint: there are almost 50.

What is:
A STRAIT? A BAY? A GULF? A FJORD? AN ESTUARY?

STRAIT—A narrow passage between two bodies of water.

BAY— A small water area enclosed on three sides by land. No appreciable mixing of fresh and salt water happens in a bay.

GULF—A very large bay.

FJORD—A long, narrow, steep, deep bay characteristic of the Scandanavian coast.

ESTUARY—A semi-enclosed place where fresh and salt water mix. Estuaries occur where rivers empty into the sea and river and ocean water mix.

Fjord, Norway

What is the COASTAL ZONE?

The Coastal Zone is a strip of land and sea starting at the high tide line and running twelve miles out to sea.

Why is the Coastal Zone important? It is the only area where fresh water meets salt water. 90+% of all ocean plants live in the coastal zone. 70+% of all ocean fish live in the coastal zone. All sand for beaches comes from, and is stored in, the coastal zone. 98% of all human ocean activity happens in the coastal zone.

The Coastal Zone is where pollution has the greatest impact on the health of our oceans.

What does SCUBA mean?

Answer:
Self
Contained
Underwater
Breathing
Apparatus.
SCUBA was invented by Jacques Cousteau in the 1940s.

How did divers breathe before SCUBA?

Divers used bulky, heavy, iron helmets ("Hardhats") with air compressors located on a ship's deck, with long air hoses dangling down to the diver.

WHERE DO BEACHES COME FROM?

BEACH SAND COMES FROM TWO SOURCES
- The action of waves crushes coastal rocks.
- Sand and gravel are carried by rivers to the coast.

BEACHES ARE ALWAYS MOVING
- Sand movement along the beach is called *litoral drift*. Litoral drift is caused by waves that hit the beach at an angle.
- Big storm waves move sand to off-shore sand bars; periods of gentle, small waves slowly push sand back on-shore to the beach.

Why are the oceans salty? Where does it come from? What's the difference between the ocean and Great Salt Lake or the Salton Sea or the Dead Sea?

Small amounts of salt flow into the oceans from rivers. Pure water evaporates from the ocean into the atmosphere, leaving the salt behind, trapped in oceans. The oceans slowly grew saltier over millions of years

Now, as much salt settles to the ocean bottom as is dumped in by rivers, so that ocean salinity is no longer changing.

Some bodies are saltier than the ocean because they are shallow, in hot climates, and are fed by saltier rivers.

San Francisco Bay

Name the Major U.S. Estuaries

Biggest U.S. Estuaries:

Chesapeake Bay

San Francisco Bay

Mississippi River Delta

Hudson River/New York Harbor

Columbia River Estuary

Delaware River

What's the biggest estuary in the world?
Answer:
Ob River Delta in N. Russia
(550 miles long, 50 miles wide)

Waves, Waves, Wonderful Waves

- **W**ind makes waves. Every wave that ever rolled across the sea was created by winds that blew across the ocean's surface.

- **W**aves don't move water. They are traveling trains of energy.

- **A**s a wave passes, water travels in a circle. That's the motion we see.

- **W**aves bend around obstacles, the way sound waves do.

- **W**aves reflect off obstacles, like light waves.

Why do waves get bigger and break at the beach?

Waves are traveling energy, often a hundred feet deep.

As a wave passes, every particle of water moves through a circle in the same way: down, back, up, and finally forward.

As the water grows shallow, the wave's energy runs into the bottom. Water is unable to move freely down and back. Wave energy is pushed up. The wave grows taller and steeper and becomes top heavy. Finally, it becomes unstable and "breaks" on the beach.

From *The Science and Math Bookmark Book.*
© 1999 Kendall Haven and Roni Berg.
Teacher Ideas Press. 1-800-237-6124

HOW DEEP IS THE OCEAN?

Pacific Ocean: 15,000 Average Depth in Feet
Atlantic Ocean: 12,000
Indian Ocean: 10,000

The deepest place in any ocean is the Marianas Trench in the western Pacific. Its depth is 35,813 ft., or 29 Empire State Buildings on top of each other!

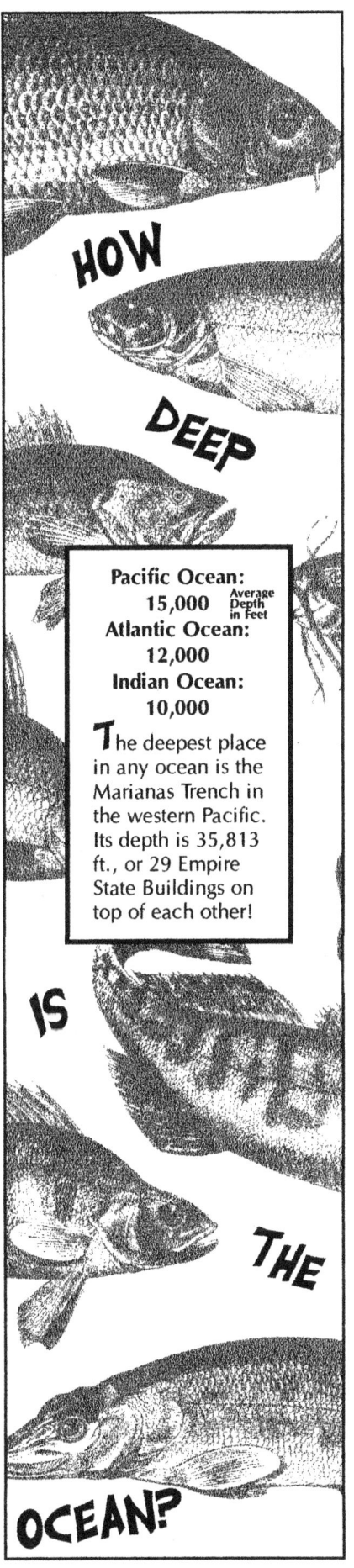

From *The Science and Math Bookmark Book.*
© 1999 Kendall Haven and Roni Berg.
Teacher Ideas Press. 1-800-237-6124

WHAT MAKES THE TIDES ROLL IN AND OUT?

The tides are really a long, single wave that sloshes back and forth across the ocean.

Tides are caused by the gravitational pull of the moon (mostly) and the sun (a little).

There are two high and two low tides each day. High tide occurs when the moon is straight above and again when the moon is on the opposite side of the earth.

The world's highest tides are in the Bay of Fundy (eastern Canada), where the tide rises 32 feet during an average tidal cycle!

The highest high tides happen every two weeks when the sun and moon are lined up to pull in the same direction. These tides are called *Spring Tides.*

From *The Science and Math Bookmark Book.*
© 1999 Kendall Haven and Roni Berg.
Teacher Ideas Press. 1-800-237-6124

WHAT IS A TSUNAMI?

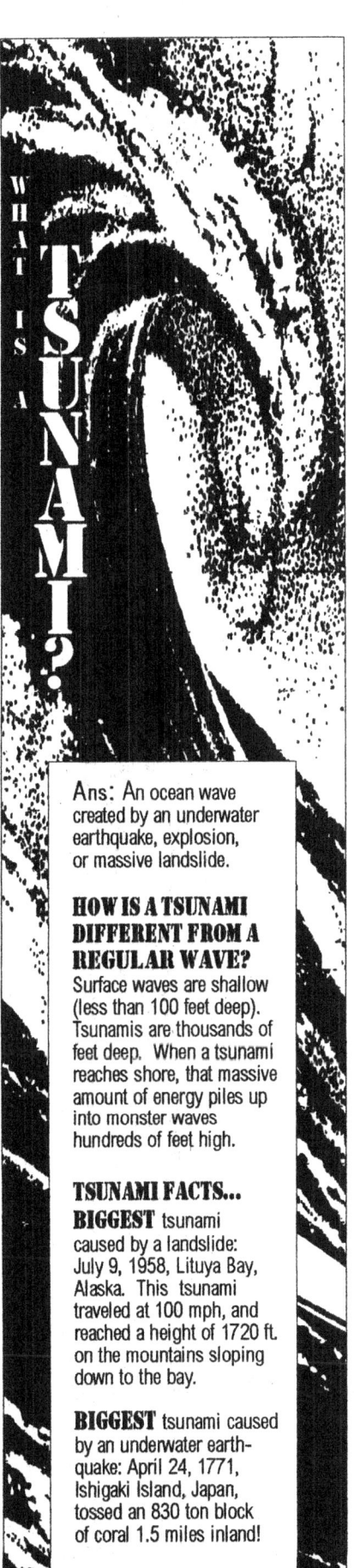

Ans: An ocean wave created by an underwater earthquake, explosion, or massive landslide.

HOW IS A TSUNAMI DIFFERENT FROM A REGULAR WAVE?

Surface waves are shallow (less than 100 feet deep). Tsunamis are thousands of feet deep. When a tsunami reaches shore, that massive amount of energy piles up into monster waves hundreds of feet high.

TSUNAMI FACTS...

BIGGEST tsunami caused by a landslide: July 9, 1958, Lituya Bay, Alaska. This tsunami traveled at 100 mph, and reached a height of 1720 ft. on the mountains sloping down to the bay.

BIGGEST tsunami caused by an underwater earthquake: April 24, 1771, Ishigaki Island, Japan, tossed an 830 ton block of coral 1.5 miles inland!

How many words do we have for "PRECIPITATION?"

Precipitation is any deposit of water that reaches the earth from the atmosphere.

Make your own list and see if you can find more than these common precipitation names.

FROZEN PRECIPITATION:
- snow
- hail
- sleet (frozen and liquid precipitation mixed)

LIQUID PRECIPITATION:
- mist (mist often settles out of fog)
- drizzle
- sprinkle
- shower
- rain
- freezing rain (a cold rain that freezes after it reaches the ground)
- downpour
- cloud burst
- deluge
- dew (Did you forget dew? It is water that settles out of the atmosphere onto the earth even though it's the only kind of precipitation that doesn't come from clouds.)

WHAT IS AN ICE AGE? WILL WE HAVE ANOTHER?

The atmosphere cools. Instead of melting, winter snows pile up year after year into thick fields of ice. Every year the cold and snow inch farther south. The sea level drops as more water is locked into thick glacial fields stretching far down from the poles. Coast lines stretch out into what used to be ocean.

THAT IS AN ICE AGE.

The last ice age ended 11,500 years ago. We are probably due for another one sometime in the next 8,000 years. Ice ages last for 20,000 to 70,000 years. Earth has been having them regularly for the last two million years.

The newest theory is that ice ages are triggered by changes in the strength and temperature of the Gulf Stream current through the North Atlantic Ocean. When the Gulf Stream pumps less heat into the northern Atlantic Ocean and to northern Europe, an ice age is triggered.

Earth Sciences 58

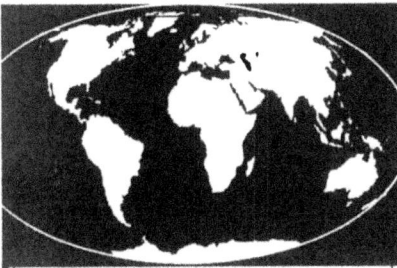

What is a Continent?

CONTINENTS ARE THE SEVEN GREAT LAND MASSES ON THE EARTH. OVER THE PAST HUNDREDS OF MILLIONS OF YEARS, THEY HAVE SMASHED TOGETHER, DRIFTED APART, AND TRAVELED OVER MUCH OF THE GLOBE.

CAN YOU NAME THE SEVEN CONTINENTS?

Australia
Antarctica
S. America
N. America
Africa
Asia
Europe

NOT INDIA. IT'S ONLY A SUB-CONTINENT.
NOT GREENLAND. IT'S ONLY AN ISLAND.

What is the Water Cycle?

Water is neither destroyed nor created, but continues to endlessly flow through a six-step cycle on our planet. The next glass of water you drink may well have water molecules that have drifted through all the oceans on Earth, fallen as rain over every continent, and have been drunk a thousand times by humans and animals over hundreds of thousands of years.

The six steps of the water cycle are:

SURFACE WATER
OCEANS
GROUND WATER
PRECIPITATION
EVAPORATION
CLOUDS

Can you put them in the correct sequential order?

Ans: oceans, evaporation, clouds, precipitation, surface water, ground water.

What Are the Names of Flowing Bodies of Fresh Water?

River: A usually high volume channel of fresh flowing water that empties into a lake, ocean, sea, or bay.

Tributary: A river that empties into another river or stream.

Stream: A small channel of fresh water that empties into any other body of water.

Bayou: A marshy stream that empties into another stream or river in the Gulf Coast and lower Mississippi River area.

Creek: A short, small tributary to a stream or river.

Brook: Any small stream.

Ground Water: A flowing river of water not visible on the surface of the ground.

WHAT ARE THE NAMES OF FRESH WATER BODIES?

Lake:
A large area of fresh water surrounded by land or by manmade dams. But there are exceptions. The Great Salt Lake is saltier than the ocean but is called a lake. Several of the Great Lakes also have significant salt content.

Reservoir:
An artificial lake created to store water for use by humans. Many American lakes should more correctly be called reservoirs.

Pond:
A small area of still water. If there is a significant current through it, it is a small lake, not a pond.

Marsh:
A tract of low-lying, usually wet, land. Most marshes are characterized by thick reeds, grasses, bogs, ponds, and streams.

Swamp:
Spongy ground largely covered by standing water of little depth.

From *The Science and Math Bookmark Book*.
© 1999 Kendall Haven and Roni Berg.
Teacher Ideas Press. 1-800-237-6124

What is soil? What is dirt?

Soil is the top few feet of the earth's crust from which humans and plants derive food and nourishment. All terrestrial life depends on soil. Every terrestrial food chain begins with soil.

WHAT IS SOIL MADE OF?
The major ingredients in soil are clay, sand, silt, and decomposed organic material called either *humus* or *loam*.

WHERE DOES NEW SOIL COME FROM?
Soil comes from two places. Dead leaves, branches, grasses and other organic material are acted on by anaerobic organisms and decomposed into soil. Rocks are pulverized and mixed with chemicals to become soil.

Dirt is a more general word that refers to soil, or to any combination of the major components of soil.

From *The Science and Math Bookmark Book*.
© 1999 Kendall Haven and Roni Berg.
Teacher Ideas Press. 1-800-237-6124

POLAR FACTS

The earth spins on its axis every day. That axis is found by drawing a line through the two poles, the North and South Poles.

BUT, that's only one set of poles. There are really *two* North Poles and *two* South Poles. The poles we think of are the *geographic* poles fixed by the lines of longitude and latitude. But there are also *magnetic* North and South Poles.

WHAT'S THE DIFFERENCE?
The magnetic poles are aligned to the earth's magnetic field. These poles drift as Earth's molten mantle and core flow and slowly shift the magnetic field. The magnetic North Pole is now over 9° away from the geographic pole.

IS IT IMPORTANT?
If you are using a compass and a map, the compass reads to the magnetic North Pole. The map is set to the geographic North Pole. Following the compass, you won't get where you want to go on the map.

From *The Science and Math Bookmark Book*.
© 1999 Kendall Haven and Roni Berg.
Teacher Ideas Press. 1-800-237-6124

WHAT'S a DESERT?

A desert is a place that will not support human life. In a practical sense, a desert is any place that gets less than 1 inch of rain each year.

Deserts change over the centuries. The vast African Sahara Desert used to be lush grassland. The Sahara is now the world's biggest desert. It is also the world's biggest sandbox.

Can you name the major U.S. deserts?

Mojave Desert
Death Valley Desert
Great Basin Desert
Painted Desert
Great Salt Lake Desert
Colorado Desert
White Sands Desert

Can you find them on a map?
(Hint: They are listed from west to east.)

From *The Science and Math Bookmark Book*.
© 1999 Kendall Haven and Roni Berg.
Teacher Ideas Press. 1-800-237-6124

What causes currents in the oceans?

Wind? No.
Wind causes waves.
Guess again.

Ocean waters flow like three-dimensional rivers. There are five forces that create the ocean currents:

1. The earth spins on its axis and forces the ocean water to flow.

2. The sun heats tropical water more than polar water, making tropical surface water lighter.

3. Evaporation cools the surface water and makes it heavier.

4. Temperature differences (thermoclines) between the Arctic surface water and ocean bottom water make the surface polar water sink.

5. Water rising along some coasts creates vertical ocean currents.

From *The Science and Math Bookmark Book*.
© 1999 Kendall Haven and Roni Berg.
Teacher Ideas Press. 1-800-237-6124

Can you name some major ocean currents?

There are more than 40 named, stable ocean currents.

Two have the greatest affect on North America:
1. GULF STREAM— flowing north along the east coast.
2. JAPAN CURRENT— flowing past Alaska and south along the west coast (sometimes called the Humboldt Current along the Pacific coast of North America).

Other major currents include:
EQUATORIAL CURRENTS— flowing across both Atlantic and Pacific oceans from east to west.
DEEP BOTTOM CURRENTS— flowing super-cold water from the poles toward the equator in both Atlantic and Pacific oceans.
SOUTHERN HEMISPHERE CURRENTS— similar to the Japan Current and Gulf Stream in the Pacific and Atlantic oceans.
ANTARCTIC CURRENTS— flowing around the Antarctic continent.

From *The Science and Math Bookmark Book*.
© 1999 Kendall Haven and Roni Berg.
Teacher Ideas Press. 1-800-237-6124

WHAT ARE TECTONIC PLATES?

The earth's surface is made of plates that float on the heavier mantle below, like the thin crust that forms on boiling fudge. These tectonic plates of the earth's surface are constantly moving.

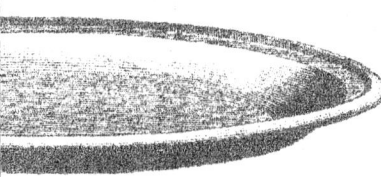

The action is at the plate boundaries, where plates crash together or rub against each other. That's where earthquakes, volcanoes, and deep ocean trenches happen. That's where new crust is created and old crust destroyed.

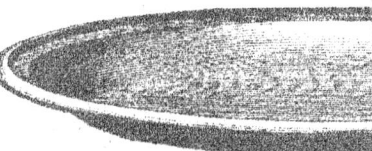

The plates and continents have drifted thousands of miles over time. Some active boundaries, like California's San Andreas fault line, move 1/4 inch per year! That's lightnin' fast for tectonic plates.

From *The Science and Math Bookmark Book.*
© 1999 Kendall Haven and Roni Berg.
Teacher Ideas Press. 1-800-237-6124

NAME THE KINDS OF OCEAN PLANTS

There are two kinds of ocean plants: the floaters and those that hook to the bottom.

The free floaters are called phytoplankton. The most common species are DIATOMS and DINOFLAGELLATES. They all live in the top layer of the ocean where there is enough sunlight to grow. They also grow mainly along coasts where upwelling brings nutrients up to them from deep ocean waters.

Kelp and ocean grasses are the plants that attach to the bottom (benthic plants). They must live along the coasts where the water is shallow enough for light to reach the bottom.

From *The Science and Math Bookmark Book.*
© 1999 Kendall Haven and Roni Berg.
Teacher Ideas Press. 1-800-237-6124

Earth Sciences 61

HAVE YOU EVER BEEN TO... THE INTER-TIDAL ZONE?

Every one who has visited the ocean shore has touched the inter-tidal zone.

The inter-tidal zone is a strip of land along the ocean shore that lies between the high tide line (how high the water gets when the tide comes in) and the low tide line (how low it gets when the tide goes out).

What's so special about the inter-tidal zone? The inter-tidal zone IS:
• home to hundreds of unique species not found anywhere else on Earth.
• biologically, the 2nd most productive land on Earth (after estuaries).
• home of tide pools, unique saltwater environments containing anemones, star fish, crabs, barnacles, clams, sea grasses, sea weeds, lichens, and countless more.
• in heavier demand for human recreation, acre for acre, than any other land on Earth.
• a fragile ecosystem that is easily destroyed.

From *The Science and Math Bookmark Book.*
© 1999 Kendall Haven and Roni Berg.
Teacher Ideas Press. 1-800-237-6124

WHAT MAMMALS LIVE IN THE OCEAN?

Only FOUR mammals live their whole lives in the ocean:
- Whale
- Porpoise
- Dolphin
- Manatee

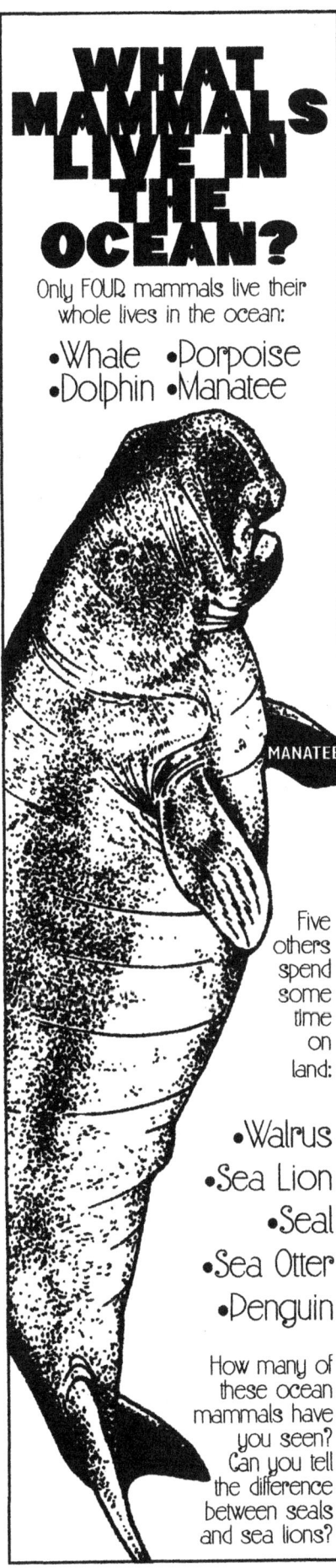

MANATEE

Five others spend some time on land:

- Walrus
- Sea Lion
- Seal
- Sea Otter
- Penguin

How many of these ocean mammals have you seen? Can you tell the difference between seals and sea lions?

From *The Science and Math Bookmark Book*.
© 1999 Kendall Haven and Roni Berg.
Teacher Ideas Press. 1-800-237-6124

Bay or Estuary? Which is Which?

Bays are semi-enclosed inlets of a sea or lake.

Estuaries are semi-enclosed bodies of water where *fresh* and *salt* water mix.

Estuaries:
- happen where rivers empty into the ocean.
- cover less than 1/100 of 1% of the earth's surface and are still the breeding ground for almost a majority of the ocean's food supply.

Estuaries are:
- nursery grounds for the ocean's food chain.
- the most biologically productive space in the world.
- home to hundreds of unique species.

Estuaries are also:
- where 15 of America's biggest cities are located.
- where most of our industrial factories are concentrated.
- in environmental danger from habitat destruction, fresh water diversion, overuse and pollution.

From *The Science and Math Bookmark Book*.
© 1999 Kendall Haven and Roni Berg.
Teacher Ideas Press. 1-800-237-6124

What's a CRUSTACEAN? Can you name any?

Crustaceans are water-dwelling animals that breathe through gills and have segmented bodies (head, thorax, and abdomen) encased in a hard exoskeleton (or shell).

The three most common crustaceans are:

LOBSTER
SHRIMP
CRAB

Sebastian in Disney's *The Little Mermaid* was a crustacean. Some Alaskan King crabs are four feet across. Some lobsters weigh forty-five pounds.

HERMIT CRAB

From *The Science and Math Bookmark Book*.
© 1999 Kendall Haven and Roni Berg.
Teacher Ideas Press. 1-800-237-6124

What is a mollusk?

Can you name any?

Mollusks are water-dwelling animals with unsegmented bodies and no vertebrae (backbones). Most mollusks live in segmented shells and have one muscled foot they use for digging, walking, and swimming.

Common mollusks:
**Snail
Mussel
Clam
Oyster
Barnacle
Octopus
Squid**

Did you know that the giant squid is the largest mollusk on Earth? Squid over 150 feet long have been caught and there is evidence that even bigger squid live in the inky-black ocean depths. Think of it. Squid tentacles longer than four school buses!

From *The Science and Math Bookmark Book.*
© 1999 Kendall Haven and Roni Berg.
Teacher Ideas Press. 1-800-237-6124

GETTING INTO THE... OZONE

Ozone is a funny molecule made up of three oxygen atoms. Normally oxygen is in molecules of only two atoms.

IN THE UPPER ATMOSPHERE:
- there is a thin layer of ozone high in the stratosphere that circles the earth.
- this ozone absorbs ultraviolet radiation and protects life on Earth from harmful UV rays.
- many modern chemicals (especially CFC's, or chloroflourocarbons– aerosol propellants) break down ozone and destroy that protective layer. Big holes and thin spots have formed in our protective ozone layer over the past 20 years.

IN THE LOWER ATMOSPHERE:
- ozone is created by car exhaust.
- ozone is one element in smog, is harmful to your health, and can kill trees.

We have too much ozone down next to the ground, and too little up in the stratosphere.

From *The Science and Math Bookmark Book.*
© 1999 Kendall Haven and Roni Berg.
Teacher Ideas Press. 1-800-237-6124

Twister

A tornado, the most violent of all storms, is a small, rapidly whirling wind storm that forms under a dark gray or black anvil-shaped thundercloud. Heavy rain and hail are common.

The average width of a tornado is less than 1000 feet at the ground and three to seven times that at the base of the clouds. Winds inside the tornado can reach as high as 500 mph. Tornadoes rarely travel faster than 35 mph.

In the very center of the swirling funnel cloud, there is an area of eerie calm.

Tornadoes are most frequent in "tornado alley," stretching from Texas through Oklahoma and Kansas into Indiana. But tornadoes have been recorded from Massachusetts to California.

Dust Devils are miniature tornadoes. Over the ocean, tornadoes are called *water spouts*.

From *The Science and Math Bookmark Book.*
© 1999 Kendall Haven and Roni Berg.
Teacher Ideas Press. 1-800-237-6124

IS A TYPHOON DIFFERENT THAN A HURRICANE OR A CYCLONE?

All three are massive, swirling storm systems with winds of 73 mph or more. Often the winds reach 130 to 150 mph. Heavy rains usually accompany the wind and storm.

If it's in the Atlantic Ocean or the Gulf of Mexico, it is called a **HURRICANE**. If it happens in the South Pacific, it is called a **TYPHOON**. Once a typhoon reaches a continental land mass, it is called a **CYCLONE**.

The Beaufort scale is used to measure the force of hurricanes and typhoons on a scale from 1 to 10. The Beaufort scale measures the size, shape, and the amount of foam and spray thrown from the waves, and the chaotic pitching of the wave peaks to determine a force number.

How much rain falls to Earth every year?

The average spot on Earth receives 34 inches of rain each year. Some places hardly get any rain. Some are flooded with hundreds of inches. But the average is 34 inches.

That is a band of water 3 feet deep covering the whole world.

How much rain is that? If you piled it up in huge boxes 1 mile long on each side and 1 mile high, you'd need 100,000 boxes to hold all that rain. If you piled those boxes on top of each other, they would reach almost half way to the moon!

If you weighed all that rain, it would weigh 752,000,000,000 tons.

Where did it all come from?

It all came from evaporation, mostly from the oceans.

What is el nino? Why does it effect our weather?

El nino is the name for a periodic, temporary warming of the surface waters in the equatorial Pacific Ocean.

El ninos usually last for only one or two years and happen every sixteen to eighteen years.

The name was created by a Chilean fisherman in the 1800's.

Changes in the surface temperature of tropical oceans alter ocean-wide circulation patterns, which change surface temperatures all over the Pacific Ocean. Changing surface temperatures change air temperature and evaporation patterns. Major air currents are shifted either a little north or south. Those seemingly small changes create big changes in the winter storm and precipitation patterns all over the world.

Life Sciences

What are the life sciences, and what do they study?

Biology: behavior, growth, and structure of living organisms.

Medical Science: functions of the human body and tissue.

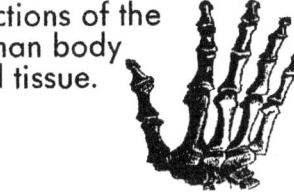

Ecology: living communities.

Anthropology: the origins, development, and distribution of humans.

Paleontology: the fossil remains of past plant and animal life.

What's the difference between an animal and a plant?

Some common guesses:
- Plants can't move. Right? Wrong. Ocean plankton can and some animals (coral and sponges) can't.

- Plants can't communicate. Right? Wrong. Many plants communicate chemically with each other.

So what is the difference?
- Animals take all their nutrients from the environment. Plants can manufacture some of their own nutrients.

- Animals grow uniformly in all parts of their body. Only certain parts of a plant grow at any given time.

It doesn't seem like much, but it's enough to classify things as either plant or animal.

HOW DO WE GROUP LIVING THINGS?

Answer: Into Kingdoms.

THERE ARE 5 KINGDOMS— Plant, Animal, Fungi, and two just for single-cell organisms.

VIRUSES aren't included in any of these kingdoms because we aren't sure if they are alive.

SOME believe viruses are the simplest of all living things. Some believe they are too simple to be called "alive." Opinion varies. They are in their own class, but it isn't rated as a kingdom.

WHAT KINDS OF THINGS ARE IN THE ANIMAL KINGDOM?

Mammal
Insect
Spider
Worm
Crustacean
Amphibian
Reptile
Fish
Bird

What kinds of things are in the Plant Kingdom?

Moss
Grass
Weed
Bush
Flower
Tree

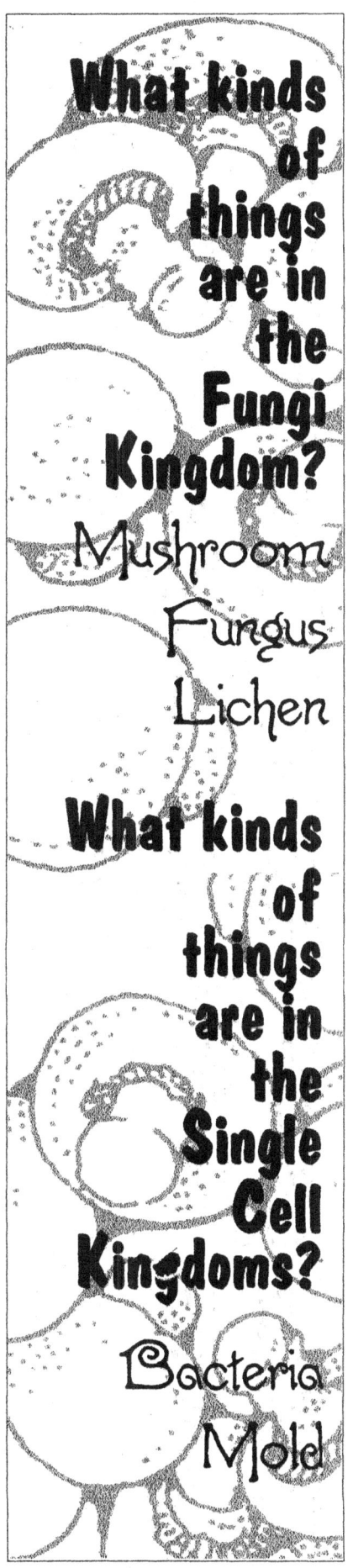

What kinds of things are in the Fungi Kingdom?

Mushroom
Fungus
Lichen

What kinds of things are in the Single Cell Kingdoms?

Bacteria
Mold

WHAT'S BELOW A KINGDOM?

There are nine levels of classification of living things: kingdom, phylum, sub-phylum, class, order, family, genus, species and individual. Kingdoms are divided into phylums, phylums into sub-phylums, and so forth. Using these nine levels of classification, scientists can uniquely identify each living thing on Earth.

Here are the levels of classification for you, a human being. Draw a line between the title of each level (left column) and the correct corresponding name (right column).

kingdom	vertebrates
phylum	you
sub-phylum	sapien
class	animal
order	homo
family	chordates
genus	hominid
species	mammal
individual	primate

Answer:
Kingdom—animal, phylum—chordates, sub-phylum—vertebrates, class—mammal, order—primate, family—hominid, genus—Homo, species—sapien, individual—YOU.

From *The Science and Math Bookmark Book.*
© 1999 Kendall Haven and Roni Berg.
Teacher Ideas Press. 1-800-237-6124

Why do scientists have to *group* everything into all those classifications and categories?

1. Scientists group species together by anatomical similarities. Every member of each group has some similiar traits.

2. Grouping by common characteristics lets them study those characteristics.

3. Grouping things helps them understand the history and evolution of life on Earth.

4. Grouping things helps them understand the role and behavior of each living species.

From *The Science and Math Bookmark Book.*
© 1999 Kendall Haven and Roni Berg.
Teacher Ideas Press. 1-800-237-6124

How many animals of each kind are there in the world?

(Numbers are estimates of individuals)

INSECTS & SPIDERS*
(ants, flies, fleas, spiders, etc.)
6,000,000,000,000,000

CRUSTACEANS
(shrimp, krill, sowbugs, etc.)
2,000,000,000,000,000

WORMS
(earthworms, ocean worms, etc.)
1,500,000,000,000,000

FISH
(ocean and fresh water)
200,000,000,000,000

MOLLUSKS
(snails, slugs, squid, etc.)
150,000,000,000,000

AMPHIBIANS
(frogs, toads, newts, etc.)
1,000,000,000,000

BIRDS
150,000,000,000

MAMMALS (excluding Humans)
(from rats to cows and pigs to elephants)
70,000,000,000

HUMANS
8,500,000,000

REPTILES
(snakes, lizards, turtles, crocodiles, etc.)
2,000,000,000

*There are a million insects for each human on earth!!!

From *The Science and Math Bookmark Book.*
© 1999 Kendall Haven and Roni Berg.
Teacher Ideas Press. 1-800-237-6124

Life Sciences 69

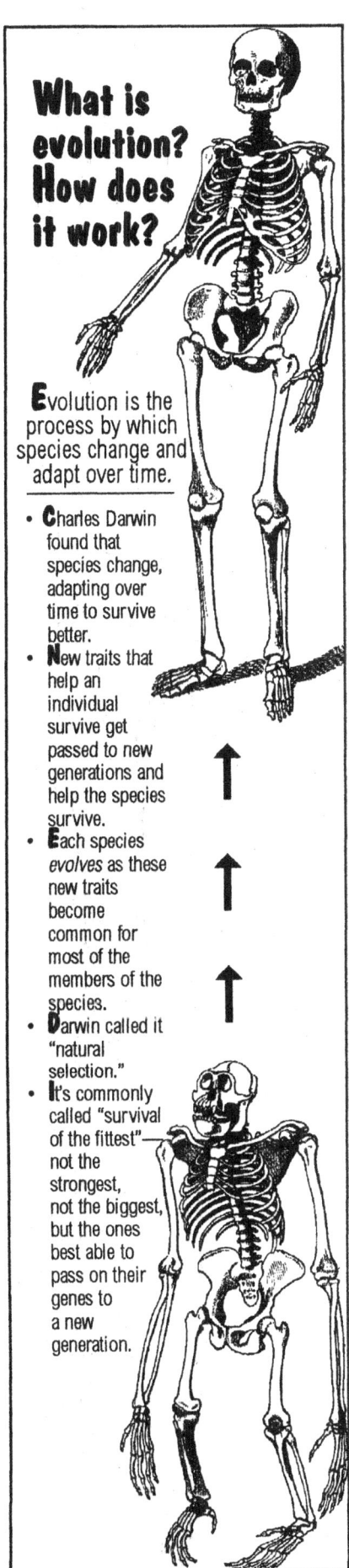

What is evolution? How does it work?

Evolution is the process by which species change and adapt over time.

- **C**harles Darwin found that species change, adapting over time to survive better.
- **N**ew traits that help an individual survive get passed to new generations and help the species survive.
- **E**ach species *evolves* as these new traits become common for most of the members of the species.
- **D**arwin called it "natural selection."
- **I**t's commonly called "survival of the fittest"—not the strongest, not the biggest, but the ones best able to pass on their genes to a new generation.

From *The Science and Math Bookmark Book*.
© 1999 Kendall Haven and Roni Berg.
Teacher Ideas Press. 1-800-237-6124

How many mythical animals can you name?

SEA SERPENT

- DRAGON
- UNICORN
- CENTAUR
- BIG FOOT
- PHOENIX
- ABOMINABLE SNOWMAN

FLYING HORSE (PEGASUS)

Are there any real animals close to any of these?

Ans: Yes. Some dolphin calls sound haunting, like reported mermaid calls. Giant squid tentacles look like sea serpents. Komodo dragons are dragon-like. So were several dinosaurs. Some goats have a unicorn-like single horn.

Can you name any more?

MERMAID

From *The Science and Math Bookmark Book*.
© 1999 Kendall Haven and Roni Berg.
Teacher Ideas Press. 1-800-237-6124

PLANT FACTS

The first life on Earth was plants (some form of algae about 3.6 billion years ago).

Ninety percent of all living matter is plants. (Only 9 percent is animal.)

Plants were on Earth 3 billion years before animals.

Only plants can create their own nutrients.

Trace any food chain back and you come to a plant.

Animals can't live without plants. Most plants would survive just fine without animals.

From *The Science and Math Bookmark Book*.
© 1999 Kendall Haven and Roni Berg.
Teacher Ideas Press. 1-800-237-6124

THE BIGGEST

Western Red Cedar

LIVING THINGS ON EARTH ARE TREES.

HOW BIG ARE THE BIGGEST TREES?

HERE ARE THE AMERICAN WINNERS:

Tree	Tallest Rank	Heaviest Rank
General Sherman Sequoia, CA	3	1*
Humbolt Coast Redwood, CA	1	2
Western Red Cedar, WA	11	3
Sitka Spruce, WA and OR	8	4
Coast Douglas Fir, OR	2	5
Bald Cyprus, LA	15	6
Sugar Pine, CA	5	9
Nobel Fir, WA	4	15

*LARGEST LIVING THING ON EARTH. IT WEIGHS 1400 TONS (THE SIZE OF 360 FULL-GROWN ELEPHANTS OR 15 MAMMOTH BLUE WHALES).

MOST COMMON U.S. TREES:

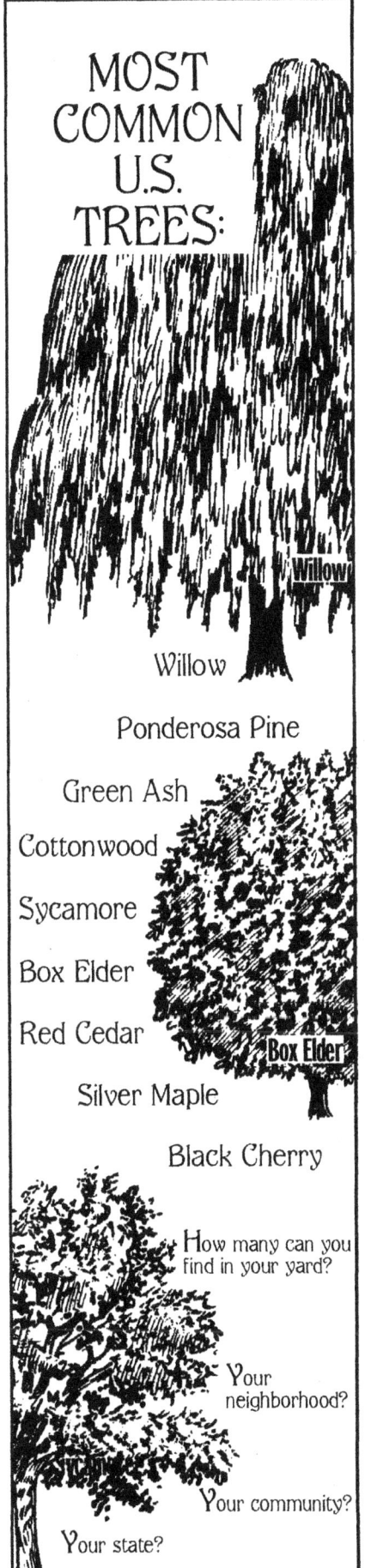

Willow
Ponderosa Pine
Green Ash
Cottonwood
Sycamore
Box Elder
Red Cedar
Silver Maple
Black Cherry

How many can you find in your yard?

Your neighborhood?

Your community?

Your state?

TREE TIDBITS

A single mutant orange tree on a Brazilian plantation in the early 1800's produced oranges without seeds. Twigs from that one tree were spliced (grafted) onto other orange trees. Parts of those trees were grafted to other trees, and so on. Every naval orange tree in the world can be traced back to that one Brazilian tree.

Every broom corn plant ever grown in America can be traced back to three seeds brought from France by Benjamin Franklin during the Revolutionary War.

an you find other trees with interesting tidbits?

Fascinating TREE Facts

Banyan trees can have hundreds of trunks (320 is the record). One banyan tree covered over 3 acres, or the area of a dozen large house lots!

Banana trees really aren't trees. Their trunk has no woody fibrous matter, just compressed shoots and a stem, like a flower.

The elephant tree of northern Mexico squirts a skunk-like, bad-smelling mist anytime one of its leaves or apricot-like fruits is pulled. It's a defensive mechanism, and it works!

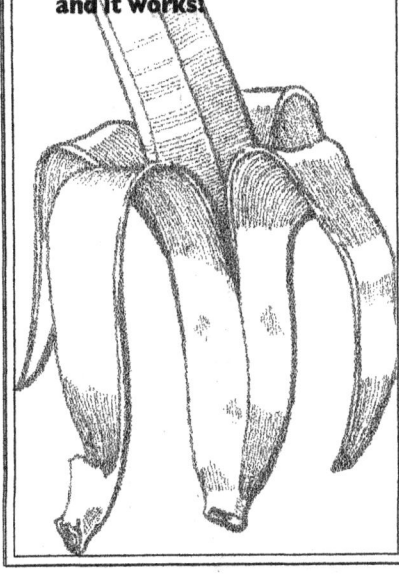

What are the BIG-GEST animals on Earth?

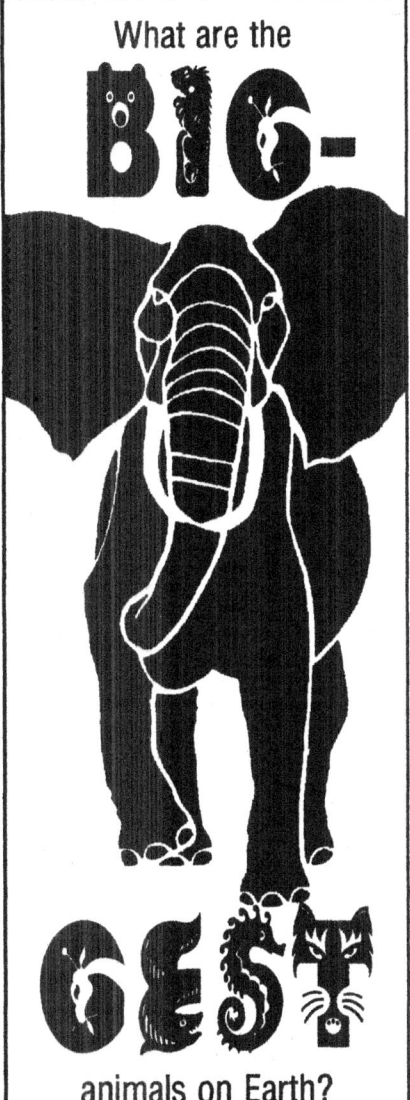

BIGGEST OF ALL
Blue Whale   110 ft., 145 tons

BIGGEST SNAKE
Anaconda   40-45 ft.

BIGGEST WORM
Tapeworm   33 ft.

BIGGEST FISH
Whale Shark   54 ft.

BIGGEST MOLLUSK
Giant Squid   200 ft., 4 tons

BIGGEST LAND ANIMAL
Elephant   24 ft., 5.5 tons

BIGGEST SPIDER
Goliath Spider   11+ inches across
                    (S. America)

BIGGEST LIZARD
Komodo Dragon 12 ft., 350 lbs.

What are the BIG-GEST carnivores on Earth?

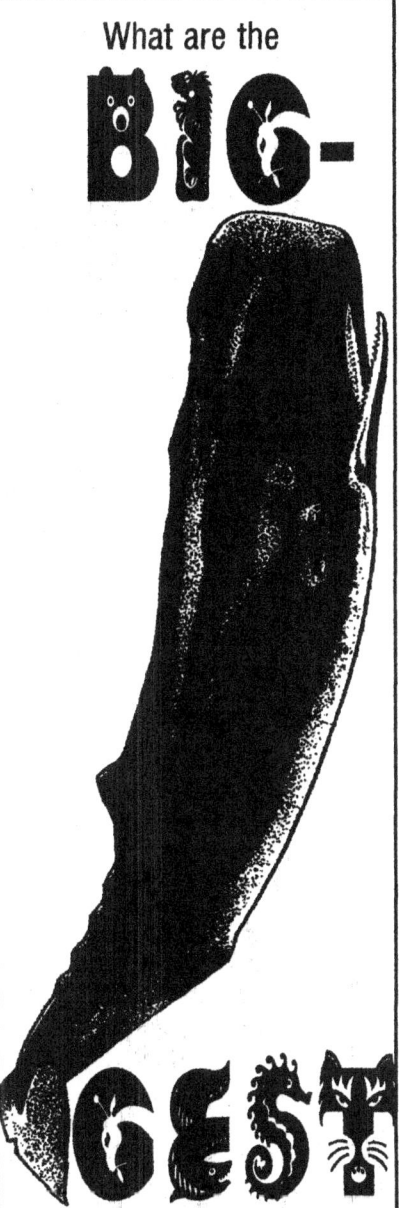

BIGGEST CARNIVORE
Sperm Whale   80 ft., 70 tons

BIGGEST LAND CARNIVORES
Elephant Seal   21 ft., 4 tons
Salt-Water Crocodile 28 ft., 2 tons
BUT, elephant seals and crocodiles live part of their lives in water.

BIGGEST ALL-LAND CARNIVORE
Grizzly Bear   12 ft., 0.75 tons
BUT, 75% of a grizzly's diet is plants.

BIGGEST TRUE LAND CARNIVORE
Siberian Tiger   12 ft., 800 pounds

Life Sciences

What are the FASTEST living things on Earth?

Cheetah	70 mph*
Sailfish	70 mph
Pronghorn Antelope	65 mph
Gazelle	58 mph
Springbok	54 mph
Marlin	52 mph
Grant's Gazelle	50 mph
Brown Hare	46 mph
Bluefin Tuna	46 mph
Race Horse	45 mph
Greyhound	43 mph
Red Deer	42 mph

SLOWEST mammal: three-toed sloth — 0.1 mph (at a full sprint). But some snails are slower than that with a top speed of 50 feet an hour, or 0.002 mph.

*Oh, you asked for the fastest? That's easy. **BIRDS**. Many birds are faster than all mammals and fish. Falcons can reach 200 mph during a diving attack. Swifts can reach 106 mph during level flight.

From *The Science and Math Bookmark Book.*
© 1999 Kendall Haven and Roni Berg.
Teacher Ideas Press. 1-800-237-6124

Pound for pound, the FASTEST, STRONGEST, most VICIOUS, and HUNGRIEST of all creatures are in the INSECT world.

- Some beetles can carry 30 times their own weight! Can you carry over 3,000 pounds?
- Fleas are the fastest jumpers in the world. They accelerate so fast, it's like going from 0 to 300 mph in one second!
- Fleas can jump a distance equal to 50 times their own body height. To match them you'd have to jump a standing broad jump of 250 feet! How close can you come?
- A praying mantis can eat its own body weight every day. Can you eat 100 pounds of food a day?

PRAYING MANTIS

From *The Science and Math Bookmark Book.*
© 1999 Kendall Haven and Roni Berg.
Teacher Ideas Press. 1-800-237-6124

WHAT ARE THE THREE AMAZING DIFFERENCES BETWEEN A SHARK AND ALL OTHER FISH?

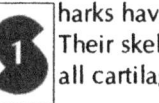 Sharks have no bones. Their skeleton is all cartilage.

 Sharks have no swim bladder (a gas-filled chamber that keeps a fish from sinking when it stops swimming).

 Sharks lack the muscles to pump water across their own gills. Gills are a fish's lungs. If a shark stops swimming, it will sink and die from lack of oxygen!

These may make sharks seem like badly designed creatures. Yet they have survived for 500 million years in the oceans—and done quite well, thank you!

From *The Science and Math Bookmark Book.*
© 1999 Kendall Haven and Roni Berg.
Teacher Ideas Press. 1-800-237-6124

POISONOUS THINGS

HOW MANY POISONOUS THINGS CAN YOU NAME? HOW MANY HAVE YOU SEEN?

SEA SNAKES
(Sea Snakes are the most toxic creatures on Earth. Most sea snakes are at least 100 times as toxic as any land snake.)

FROGS
(Frogs are the most poisonous land animal, especially small South and Central American frogs.)

LAND SNAKES
(There are over 50 species of poisonous snakes. The bushmaster and mamba are the most deadly.)

JELLY FISH
SPIDERS
SCORPIONS
OCEAN FISH
(Two have poisonous bites, and several more are poisonous if you try to eat them.)

PLANTS
(Poison ivy, poison oak, oleander and pyracantha are the best known poisonous plants.)

SEA ANEMONES and CORALS
(Some are poisonous.)

BUT, there are no poisonous mammals, birds, or fresh water fish....Any ideas why?

From *The Science and Math Bookmark Book*.
© 1999 Kendall Haven and Roni Berg.
Teacher Ideas Press. 1-800-237-6124

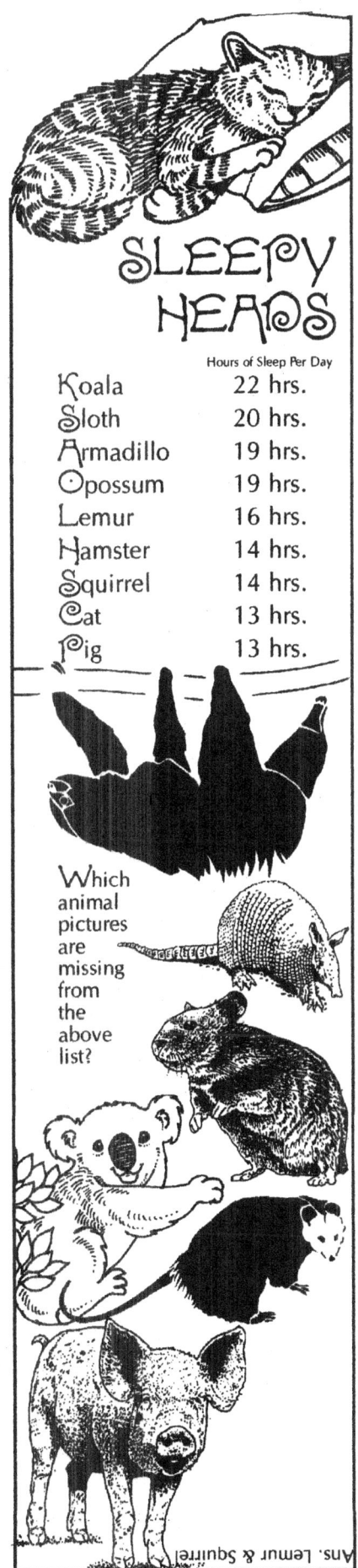

SLEEPY HEADS

Hours of Sleep Per Day

Koala	22 hrs.
Sloth	20 hrs.
Armadillo	19 hrs.
Opossum	19 hrs.
Lemur	16 hrs.
Hamster	14 hrs.
Squirrel	14 hrs.
Cat	13 hrs.
Pig	13 hrs.

Which animal pictures are missing from the above list?

Ans. Lemur & Squirrel

From *The Science and Math Bookmark Book*.
© 1999 Kendall Haven and Roni Berg.
Teacher Ideas Press. 1-800-237-6124

What is an Ecosystem?

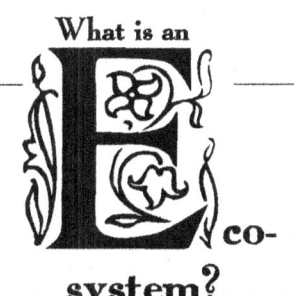

Answer:
An ecosystem is the combination of plants, animals, land, and weather of a geographic area.

Ecosystems are self-supporting. Whatever food or nutrients any member of the ecosystem needs are produced by some other part of the ecosystem. Only water and sunlight come into the ecosystem from outside the system.

ARE YOU PART OF AN ECOSYSTEM?
Certainly. You interact with your environment and the living things in it within the defined geographical area where you live.

From *The Science and Math Bookmark Book*.
© 1999 Kendall Haven and Roni Berg.
Teacher Ideas Press. 1-800-237-6124

Life Sciences 74

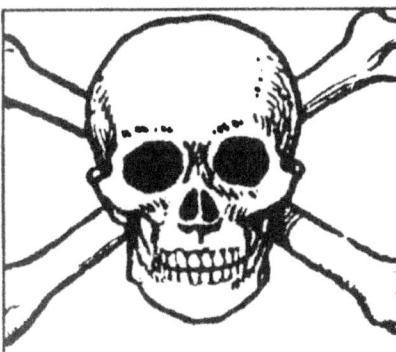

WHAT CURRENTLY THREATENS NATURAL ECOSYSTEMS?

- ACID RAIN
- PESTICIDES
- URBAN RUNOFF
- PETRO-CHEMICAL DISCHARGE
- PETROLEUM SPILLS
- TOXIC DUMPING OF TRASH AND GARBAGE
- GREENHOUSE WARMING
- SMOG— SULFUR OXIDES AND NITROUS OXIDES
- HABITAT DESTRUCTION

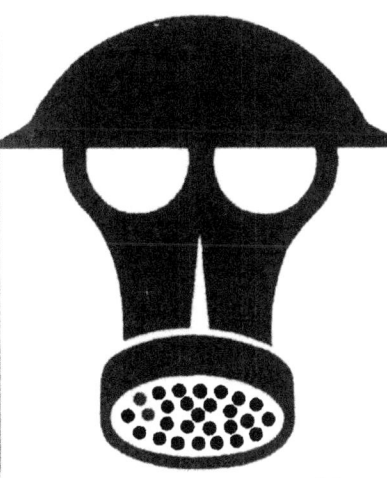

Which of these are caused by humans? All of them!

From *The Science and Math Bookmark Book.*
© 1999 Kendall Haven and Roni Berg.
Teacher Ideas Press. 1-800-237-6124

A human is alive.
A bamboo hat is not.
Is mold alive?
Is a fungus alive?
Is a virus alive?

To be called alive, an organism must meet all of the following four tests. Do you pass?

1 Chemical reactions must occur inside its cells.

2 It must be capable of reproducing itself.

3 It must have a physical boundary—a cell membrane, skin, bark, etc.

4 The organism must take in matter from the environment (breathe, eat, drink) and pass some matter back out to the environment (exhale, perspire, expel waste products).

If you do all four of these, you're ALIVE.

Ans. Mold and Fungus...yes.
Virus....some scientists say yes, some no.

From *The Science and Math Bookmark Book.*
© 1999 Kendall Haven and Roni Berg.
Teacher Ideas Press. 1-800-237-6124

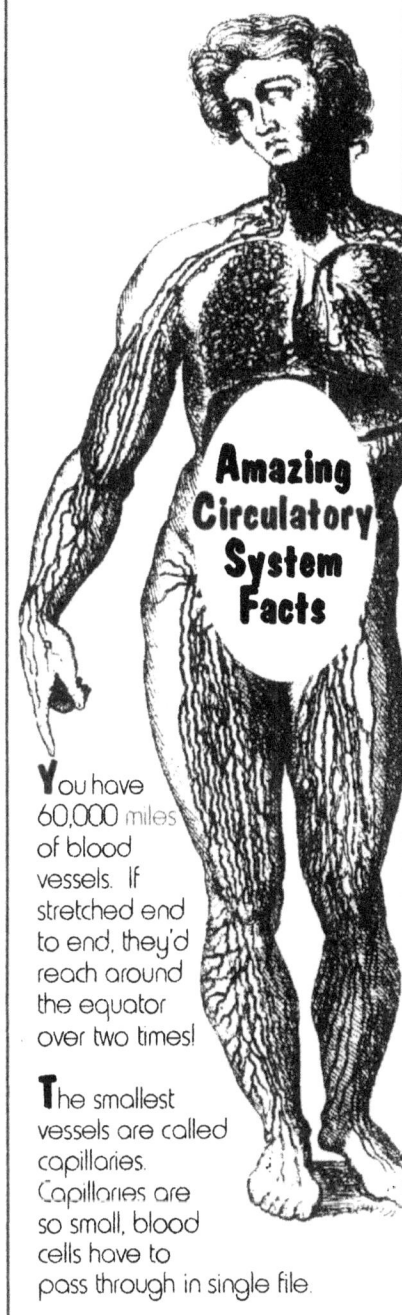

Amazing Circulatory System Facts

You have 60,000 miles of blood vessels. If stretched end to end, they'd reach around the equator over two times!

The smallest vessels are called capillaries. Capillaries are so small, blood cells have to pass through in single file.

There are more than 40,000,000,000 capillaries in your body.

There are more paths in your circulatory system than roads in all of the United States!

The biggest blood vessels are the arteries and veins leading into and out of the heart.

Blue whales' arteries are so big, a 20-pound salmon could comfortably swim through them.

From *The Science and Math Bookmark Book.*
© 1999 Kendall Haven and Roni Berg.
Teacher Ideas Press. 1-800-237-6124

Facts about Blood

Your blood delivers oxygen and all needed nutrients to each of your body's cells, and hauls away all the garbage and waste.

Your blood carries your protective police force, which destroys invading germs, viruses, and bacteria that would do you harm.

A grown human has about five quarts of blood.

Your bones (actually bone marrow) make new blood cells to replace ones that are lost or die.

HEART FACTS

Your circulation system has only one pump to power the flow of all your blood through all your blood vessels: the heart.

Your heart will beat almost 3 billion times during your lifetime.

The heart has three electrical pace makers to keep it beating on time.

Sometimes all three fail and a person needs an artificial pace maker.

Your heart has four chambers— two for incoming blood, two for outgoing blood.

The heart works by squeezing its chambers and increasing the pressure of the blood inside. This squirts the blood through the arteries, to the capillaries, and back to the heart through veins.

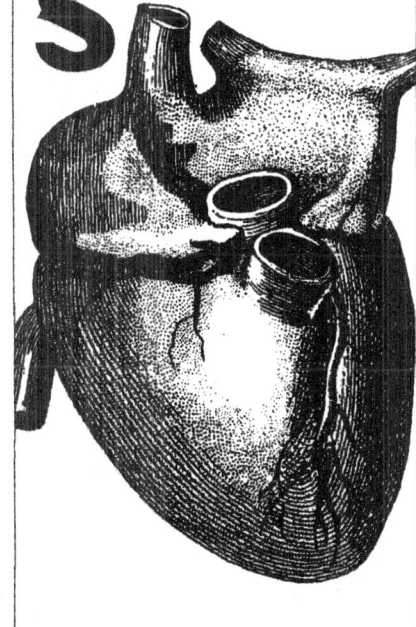

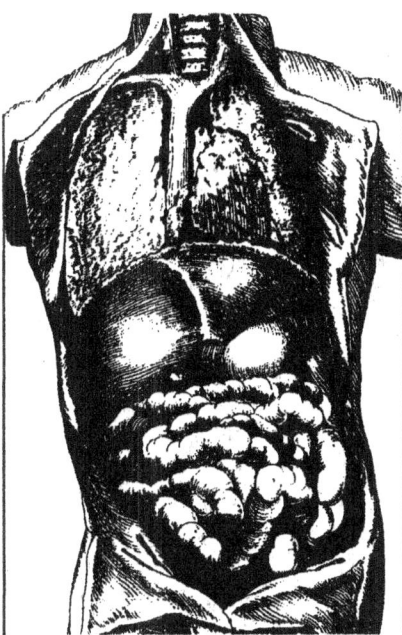

Where does your blood go?

What parts of your body get how much of the blood that's pumping through you?

Organ	Resting %	Exercise %
Heart	3	9
Brain	13	11
Kidneys	20	5
Digestive	27	7
Skeletal Muscles	15	51
Skin	9	14
Bones	5	2
All Other	8	1

That's why you shouldn't exercise right after eating. The blood your digestive system needs gets pulled away to the skeletal muscles.

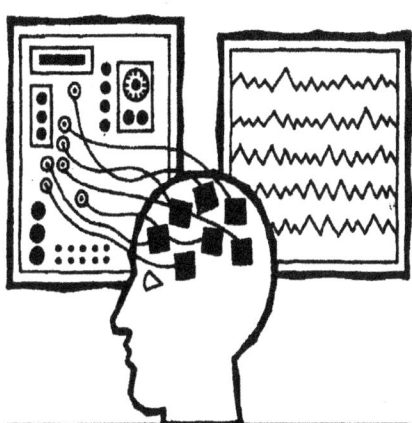

THE ELECTRIC TRUTH ABOUT THE NERVOUS SYSTEM

Your nervous system is your body's communication system, your private phone system.

Every bit of information you get goes to the brain through the nervous system. Every command from the brain does too.

As good as it is, your nervous system passes information 1000 times slower than even slow computers.

Your nervous system is part electrical and part chemical.

What is a neuron?

 THE WIRES OF YOUR NERVOUS SYSTEM ARE THE NERVE CELLS, CALLED NEURONS. LIKE TELEPHONE WIRES, THEY CARRY ALL OF YOUR BODY'S COMMUNICATIONS. THEY RANGE FROM 1/4 INCH LONG TO OVER THREE FEET!

INSIDE NEURONS, SIGNALS ZIP ALONG AS ELECTRICAL IMPULSES. BUT NEURONS DON'T HOOK DIRECTLY TO EACH OTHER AS DO WIRES IN AN ELECTRICAL CIRCUIT. THERE IS A TINY GAP BETWEEN NEURONS, OFTEN LESS THAN ONE MILLIONTH OF AN INCH WIDE. TO CROSS THAT GAP, ELECTRICAL SIGNALS ARE CONVERTED TO CHEMICAL REACTIONS WHICH SHUTTLE ACROSS THE GAP TO SPARK ELECTRICAL SIGNALS IN THE NEXT NEURON.

UNLIKE ELECTRICAL WIRES, NEURONS ARE SPECIALIZED. SOME ONLY CARRY PAIN INFORMATION, OR PRESSURE, OR HOT/COLD, ETC.

DO ALL SIGNALS GO TO THE BRAIN?

Not all signals go to the brain for interpretation and action. Some signals involving great physical danger zip to reflex centers to create fast motor-muscle responses. Then the brain is sent a memo later of what happened.

Example: Pulling your finger off a hot stove or off a rose thorn that has stabbed you.

Life Sciences 77

THE NOSE KNOWS

THE NERVOUS SYSTEM AT WORK ON YOUR NOSE.

[1] Something tickles your nose. Nerve endings on the tip of your nose send an electrical distress signal to the brain.

[2] The message passes through five neurons and four chemical gaps in four nanoseconds, reaching the brain processor.

[3] The brain compares this signal to others it has received and decides it is an itch.

[4] From memory banks, the brain retrieves the appropriate remedy.

[5] A message is dispatched to the conscious brain, informing it that a nose itch has been recorded and is being handled.

[6] At the same time, action signals are sent to shoulder, arm, wrist, and finger muscles to scratch the itch.

[7] Signals are sent to all parts of the skeletal muscles to maintain body balance and compensate for this arm movement.

[8] One finger scratches the itchy nose.

[9] Nerve endings send back a message that the itch has ceased.

[10] The brain sends signals to all muscles to cancel the itch alert.

From *The Science and Math Bookmark Book.*
© 1999 Kendall Haven and Roni Berg.
Teacher Ideas Press. 1-800-237-6124

THE HEART OF THE NERVOUS SYSTEM ...THE BRAIN!

- **Your** brain weighs only three pounds.
- **Still** it is the most complex, powerful computer ever devised. Your brain can out-think room-sized, multi-million dollar computers.
- **A** brain can reason, interpret, evaluate, and compare dissimilar things. Computers can't.
- **Your** brain contains over 100,000,000 neurons.
- **There** are more possible pathways through this neuron net than there are particles in the universe!

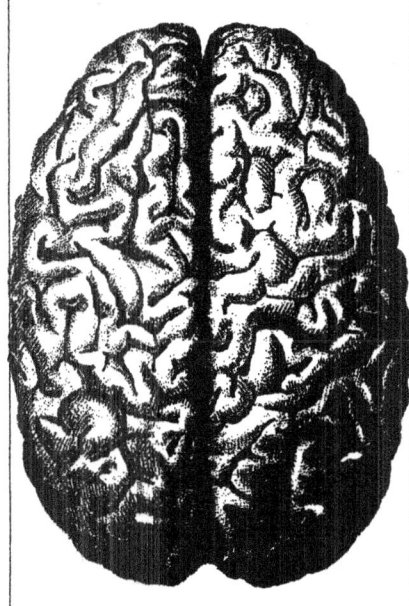

From *The Science and Math Bookmark Book.*
© 1999 Kendall Haven and Roni Berg.
Teacher Ideas Press. 1-800-237-6124

the Inner Ear

IF YOUR BRAIN CAN ONLY RECEIVE ELECTRICAL SIGNALS, HOW CAN YOU HEAR SOUNDS?

Like a telephone, your ear turns mechanical vibration into electrical pulses.

Sound waves vibrate the ear drum.

Three middle ear bones amplify the vibration 20 times louder than they received it and pass the vibrations to the fluid-filled inner ear.

Tiny hairs in the inner ear vibrate with this sloshing liquid. They convert physical vibration into **ELECTRICAL** pulses. These pulses travel along neurons to be interpreted by the brain.

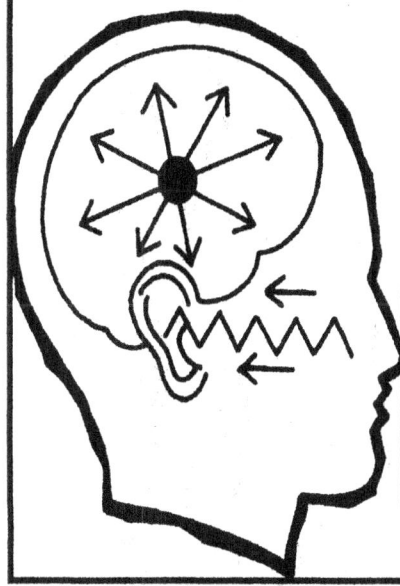

From *The Science and Math Bookmark Book.*
© 1999 Kendall Haven and Roni Berg.
Teacher Ideas Press. 1-800-237-6124

Life Sciences 78

WHY DO YOU NEED TWO EARS AND TWO EYES?

Two ears can detect direction to a sound by comparing the loudness in each ear.

Two eyes can detect distance to an object by comparing images from each eye.

Not all ears are on animal's heads. Spiders and crickets hear through their legs. Scorpions hear through their abdomen.

Your body's BIGGEST and Smallest

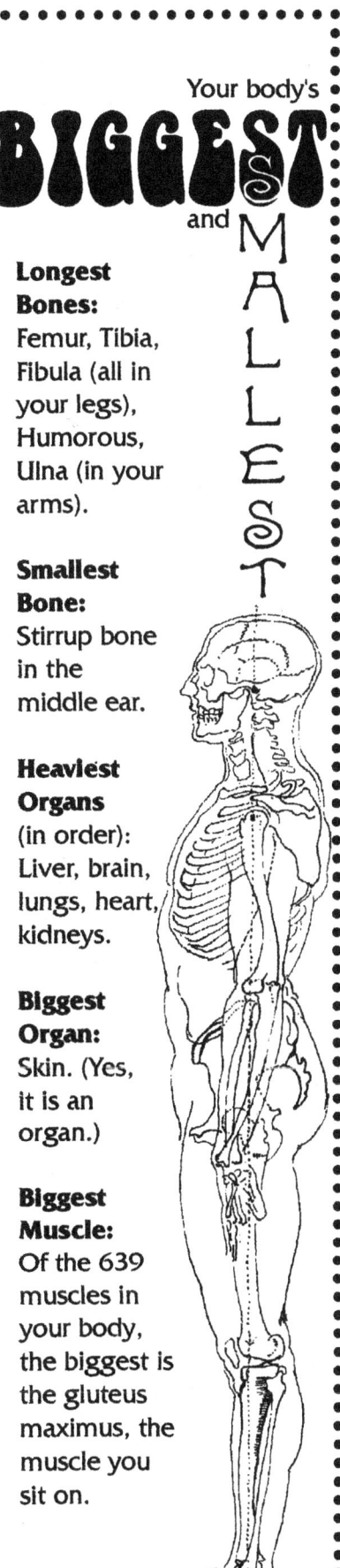

Longest Bones: Femur, Tibia, Fibula (all in your legs), Humorous, Ulna (in your arms).

Smallest Bone: Stirrup bone in the middle ear.

Heaviest Organs (in order): Liver, brain, lungs, heart, kidneys.

Biggest Organ: Skin. (Yes, it is an organ.)

Biggest Muscle: Of the 639 muscles in your body, the biggest is the gluteus maximus, the muscle you sit on.

CELL FACTS

▼ THERE ARE 10 TRILLION **CELLS** IN YOUR BODY.

▼ **CELLS** ARE LIKE FACTORIES, OR EVEN CITIES.

▼ **CELLS** CONVERT MATTER TO ENERGY JUST LIKE AN ENERGY FACTORY.

▼ **CELLS** ALSO ORDER SUPPLIES FROM THE BLOOD. THEY INVENTORY AND STORE RAW MATERIALS. THEY PROCESS MATERIALS INTO ENERGY. THEY TRANSPORT THE WASTE TO PICK-UP PORTS FOR THE BLOOD TO CARRY AWAY—JUST LIKE A BIG FACTORY!

▼ EACH **CELL** PERFORMS MILLIONS OF CHEMICAL REACTIONS EACH SECOND.

AMAZING, ISN'T IT? YOU PROBABLY DIDN'T KNOW YOU COULD DO ALL THAT.

WHAT'S INSIDE A CELL?

One human cell has more parts and carries out more activity than many small countries.

There are four general parts to a cell:

NUCLEUS — makes decisions and tells everyone what to do.

CHEMICAL FACTORY — where the real work is performed.

TRANSPORTATION SYSTEM — stores material and moves it in and out.

SKIN (or membrane) — protects the cell and handles shipping and receiving.

From *The Science and Math Bookmark Book.*
© 1999 Kendall Haven and Roni Berg.
Teacher Ideas Press. 1-800-237-6124

WHAT'S IN THE NUCLEUS OF A CELL?

The cell nucleus carries your genetic blueprint and operating instructions. Scientists call this plan your DNA. This incredible chemical code tells every cell and every part of every cell exactly what to do and when to do it. DNA is the operating manual for your body.

From *The Science and Math Bookmark Book.*
© 1999 Kendall Haven and Roni Berg.
Teacher Ideas Press. 1-800-237-6124

Nutrition Quiz

1. A two-ounce chocolate bar is the nutritional equivalent of four teaspoons of oil or butter plus 10 teaspoons of sugar? True or False
Ans. True

2. Is there any fat in unbuttered, movie-theatre popcorn?
Ans. A large bucket of unbuttered popcorn popped in coconut oil has three-days' worth of artery-clogging fat.

3. Is apple juice more nutritious than orange juice?
Ans. No. Orange juice has 50 times more vitamin C, 170 percent more folic acid, and 50 percent more potassium than apple juice.

4. How many POUNDS of potato chips, pretzels, tortilla and corn chips, popcorn, nuts, and other salty snacks does a typical American eat in a year? a. 4 b. 12 c. 17 d. 21
Ans. 21

5. Which has more vitamin C?
a. one medium stalk of broccoli b. one cup of orange juice c. one baked chicken drumstick
Ans. BROCCOLI (162 mg. vitamin C) ORANGE JUICE (120 mg. vitamin C) CHICKEN (No vitamin C)

6. All wheat breads are more nutritious than white breads. True or False
Ans. False. Some wheat breads are just white bread colored with caramel. The most fiber and nutrients are in bread made with whole grains, such as whole wheat or whole rye, etc.

From *The Science and Math Bookmark Book.*
© 1999 Kendall Haven and Roni Berg.
Teacher Ideas Press. 1-800-237-6124

Your Mighty Muscles

- CAN muscles push? No! All they can do is contract (pull).
- YOUR body has over 600 muscles divided into two groups:
  1. SKELETAL MUSCLES move the bones around.
  2. SMOOTH MUSCLES help organs (stomach, intestines, heart, blood vessels, etc.) do their job.
- SKELETAL muscles attach to tendons, which attach to bones. Skeletal muscles contract, pull the bones, and move you.
- HALF the total weight of an average adult is muscle.
- WHEN we say "make a muscle," which muscle do you tighten? Ans: the striated muscle. (We commonly call it the biceps.)
- WHAT muscle do you use the most? Ans: the heart muscle. It never gets a break as other muscles do, but works constantly all your life.

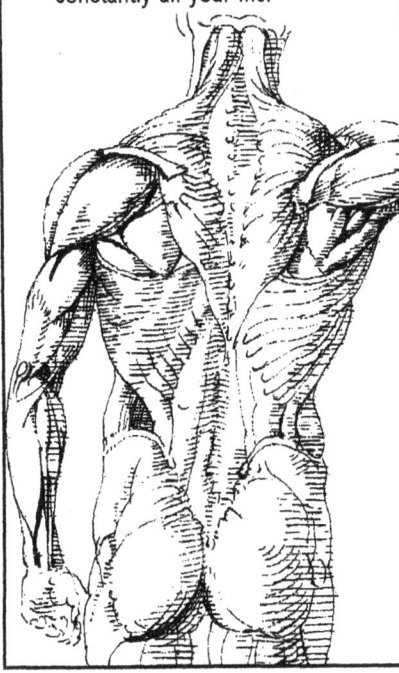

From *The Science and Math Bookmark Book.*
© 1999 Kendall Haven and Roni Berg.
Teacher Ideas Press. 1-800-237-6124

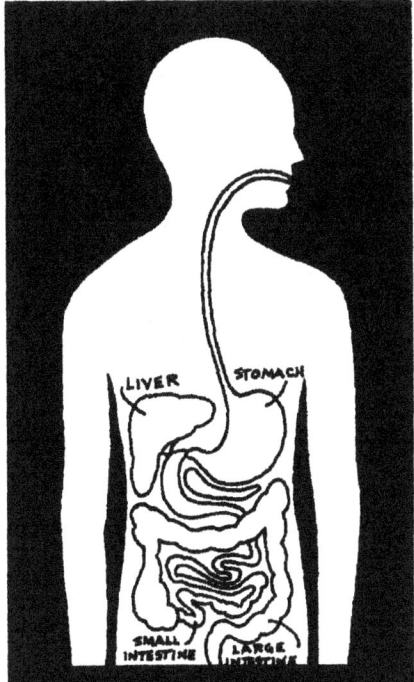

DIGEST THIS!

You eat pizza, but your cells can't. They need glucose (sugar), carbohydrates, proteins, minerals, and vitamins. Your digestive system converts the pizza you eat into the nutrient forms your body needs, and gets rid of the things you eat that your body doesn't want.

DO YOU KNOW THE PARTS OF THE DIGESTIVE SYSTEM?

- Mouth (teeth, tongue, and saliva glands)
- Esophagus
- Stomach
- Gall bladder
- Pancreas
- Small intestine
- Large intestine
- Colon

Your digestive system digests, breaks down and processes over 1/2 a ton of food each year!

Your digestive system also releases chemicals to tell the brain it's time to eat. That's what makes you hungry.

From *The Science and Math Bookmark Book.*
© 1999 Kendall Haven and Roni Berg.
Teacher Ideas Press. 1-800-237-6124

WHAT IS A LIVER?

YOUR LIVER is so essential that you have eight times as much liver as you actually need. If the liver goes, you go.

YOUR AMAZING LIVER performs over 500 separate chemical functions for you—all without having to be asked!

YOUR LIVER
- converts some substances into more useful forms. (It makes essential stuff.)
- removes a host of impurities from your blood. (It's your body's oil filter.)
- stores many important vitamins and minerals for later use. (It's a vitamin warehouse.)

TWO DISEASES strike the liver.
- hepatitis
- cirrhosis

From *The Science and Math Bookmark Book.*
© 1999 Kendall Haven and Roni Berg.
Teacher Ideas Press. 1-800-237-6124

WHAT IS A HEART ATTACK? CAN YOU HAVE A BRAIN ATTACK?

Heart attacks happen when a blood clot suddenly blocks blood flow to a coronary artery. The culprit behind these attacks is long-term buildup of fatty deposits along the walls of the arteries that severely narrow the artery opening.

If blood flow is interrupted to the heart muscles and to the nerve fibers that control them, those muscles stop working. That's a heart attack.

If the clot blocks an artery in the brain instead of in the heart, it is called a stroke. Some brain function is lost instead of heart muscle function being lost. Heart attacks and strokes are the same kind of event, just in different parts of the body.

Why do you SLEEP? Why do you DREAM?

You sleep about 1/3rd of your life (8 hrs. a day, or almost 3000 hrs. a year). If you live to be 100 years old, you will have slept over 12,000 days!

No one knows for sure why we need to sleep, but sleep seems to let the brain put itself back in order, restock itself with hormones, and reorganize itself.

During sleep we dream. No one knows for sure why we dream. The best current guess is that dreams are the brain's attempt to organize data and to mull over what has happened during the day. But maybe dreams are just the brain dumping useless electrical trash or dreams are messages from your subconscious mind. No one knows for sure.

The Amazing DNA

DNA is the short name for deoxyribonucleic acid. DNA is the genetic blueprint for your body.

DNA is a molecule shaped like a long, spiral staircase, two intertwined corkscrews with chemical bonds, like stairs, linking them together.

A copy of your DNA molecule exists in the nucleus of every cell in your body.

YOUR DNA contains billions of chemically encoded instructions directing how every part of your body will look, grow, and develop over the course of your life.

EVERY living organism (plant or animal) has a DNA molecule. They are all structured the same. Much of the double-helix spiral DNA molecule looks the same for every species. Even a lowly bacteria has DNA that looks very much like yours.

THE structure of our DNA was discovered in 1953 by Francis Crick (English) and James Watson (American).

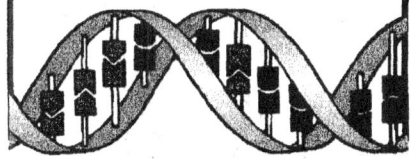

Some Nutrient Friends of Your Body:

Protein
Proteins are the molecular workhorses of life. Proteins digest food, form skin, create cell membranes, carry oxygen and iron in the blood, and do a host of other important functions that rebuild your cells and tissues.

Carbohydrates
Carbohydrates (starches and sugars) are our source of energy. However, excess carbohydrates turn into fat for storage in our body.

Fat
Fat is stored energy. We need some fat in our bodies and diets. The problem is that we get way too much fat.

Vitamins
Vitamins are essential trace organic chemical compounds. They include 13 vitamins: A, B complex, C, D, E, G, H, K, biotin, niacin, and pantothenic acid.

Minerals
Minerals are trace elements we need a little bit of and can't get by without—like zinc, potassium, iron, magnesium, iodine, and copper. Interestingly, many essential minerals are deadly toxins in larger amounts.

Vitamin Quiz A

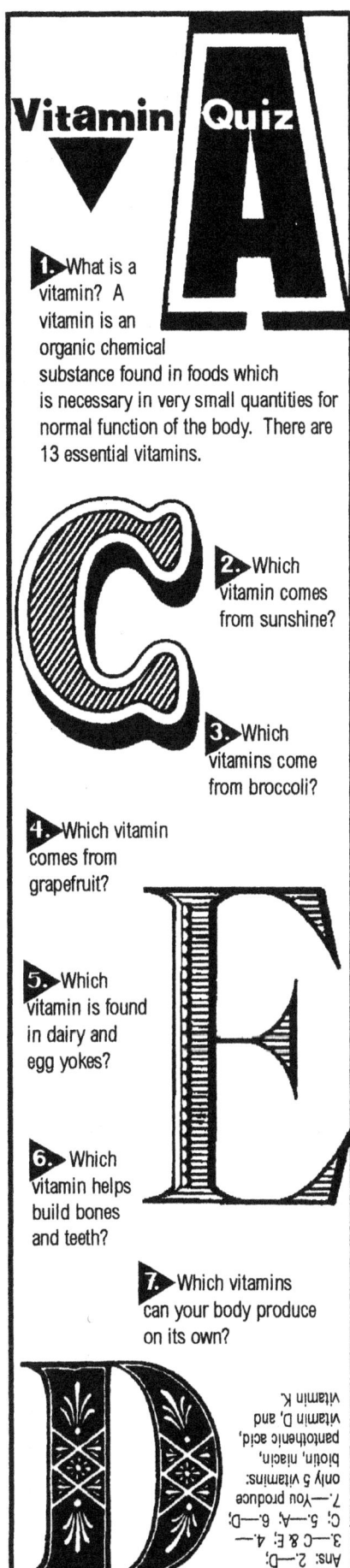

1. What is a vitamin? A vitamin is an organic chemical substance found in foods which is necessary in very small quantities for normal function of the body. There are 13 essential vitamins.

2. Which vitamin comes from sunshine?

3. Which vitamins come from broccoli?

4. Which vitamin comes from grapefruit?

5. Which vitamin is found in dairy and egg yokes?

6. Which vitamin helps build bones and teeth?

7. Which vitamins can your body produce on its own?

Ans: 2.—D; 3.—C & E; 4.—C; 5.—A; 6.—D; 7.—You produce only 5 vitamins: biotin, niacin, pantothenic acid, vitamin D, and vitamin K.

Your immune system—your private army.

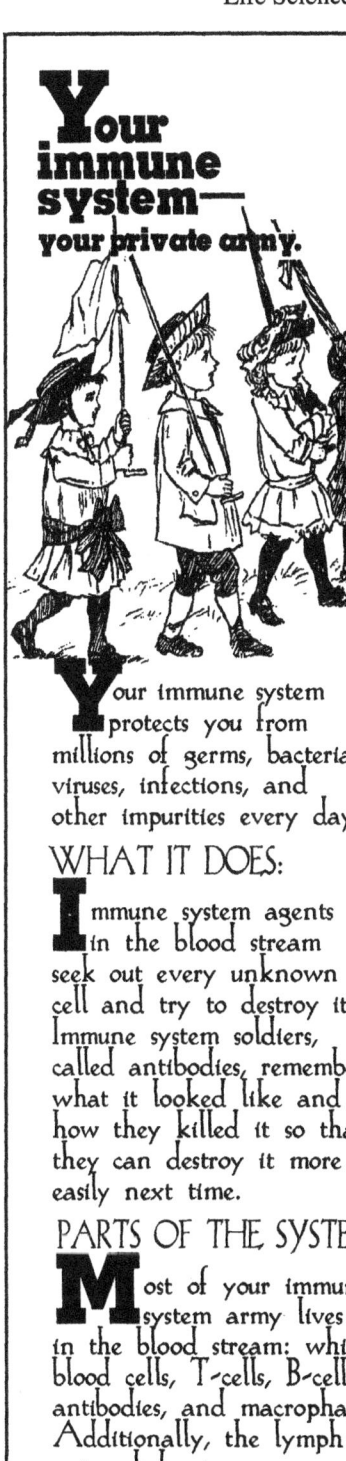

Your immune system protects you from millions of germs, bacteria, viruses, infections, and other impurities every day.

WHAT IT DOES:
Immune system agents in the blood stream seek out every unknown cell and try to destroy it. Immune system soldiers, called antibodies, remember what it looked like and how they killed it so that they can destroy it more easily next time.

PARTS OF THE SYSTEM:
Most of your immune system army lives in the blood stream: white blood cells, T-cells, B-cells, antibodies, and macrophages. Additionally, the lymph system helps to carry away invading cells after they have been killed.

WHEN IT RUNS AMOK:
Often the immune system does its job so well it begins to attack you. Diseases associated with an overactive immune system include: allergies, arthritis, and rheumatic fever.

TRANSFUSION

WHAT TYPE OF BLOOD ARE YOU?

↗ **THERE** are five general types of blood: A, B, O, A2 and AB. Also, a factor, the Rh factor, can either be positive (+) or negative (-). Thus, there are ten kinds of human blood.

↗ **BLOOD** types were discovered by Doctor Karl Landsteiner in 1897.

↗ **WHICH** type is most common?

BLOOD TYPE	% OF US THAT HAVE IT
O+	40%
A+	35%
B+	8%
A2+	7%
O-	7%
A-	0.6%
AB+	0.6%
B-	0.6%
A2-	0.6%
AB-	0.6%

↗ **WHAT** blood type are you?

↗ **WHY** do we care?

↗ **NOT** all blood types are compatible. If you get a transfusion of the wrong type of blood, you could die. It used to happen all the time.

YOUR SCARY SKELETON

WHAT DOES YOUR SKELETON DO?

It gives **SHAPE** to your body.

IT HOLDS YOUR BODY UP LIKE THE WOODEN FRAMING OF A HOUSE OR THE METAL GIRDERS OF AN OFFICE BUILDING.

IT PROTECTS IMPORTANT INTERNAL ORGANS.

THE CENTER (MARROW) OF YOUR MAJOR SKELETAL BONES PRODUCE ALL YOUR RED BLOOD CELLS.

WHAT'S IN A SKELETON?

- **Y**our skeleton includes 206 bones.
- **M**ore than 60 are in your hands, wrists and arms.
- **T**he smallest bone is the tiny stirrup bone of the middle ear.
- **T**he largest is the femur, or thigh bone.
- **T**he heaviest is the skull.
- **M**ost people have 12 ribs on each side. But some people have an extra one, and some are missing one and only have 11.
- **L**igaments hold the bones together.
- **C**artilage separates the bones and keeps them from rubbing against each other.

Tooth Talk

How many teeth do young children have?
Ans: 20. 8 molars, 4 canines, and 8 incisors.

How many do adults have?
Ans: 32. 12 molars, 8 premolars, 4 canines, and 8 incisors.

Chew on This?

- CANINES are designed to grab and hold food.
- INCISORS are designed to tear or cut off a bite.
- MOLARS and premolars are designed to grind up food and begin the digestive process.
- The third (last) molar is called the wisdom tooth. Ancient folklore claimed that this tooth was associated with improved wisdom.
- Did you know that tooth enamel is the hardest substance in your body?

Most Common Tooth Problems:

1. Cavities or tooth decay.
2. Spacing, growth direction, and placement (corrected by braces and wisdom teeth removal).
3. Gum disease.

The Human Factory

Industrial factories bring in raw materials, use heat and chemical processes to change them into new products or services, and ship out all the waste products they create.

Your body is the same. Every day you bring in new supplies of raw materials to your body-factory (food, water and air). Your body systems chemically convert these raw materials to power the work of your cells.

Factories have transportation systems. Your body has a blood system.

Factories have communications systems. Your body has a nervous system.

Factories have storage facilities to store fuel and extra products. Your body has fat cells to store extra energy and a liver to store some vitamins and minerals.

Factories have administrative headquarters. Your body has a brain.

Factories have waste management systems. Your body has systems to process solid and liquid waste and used air.

Even more amazing, every cell in your body also performs every one of these functions. Each of your billions of cells acts like its own complex factory!

Name the BIGGEST dinosaurs:

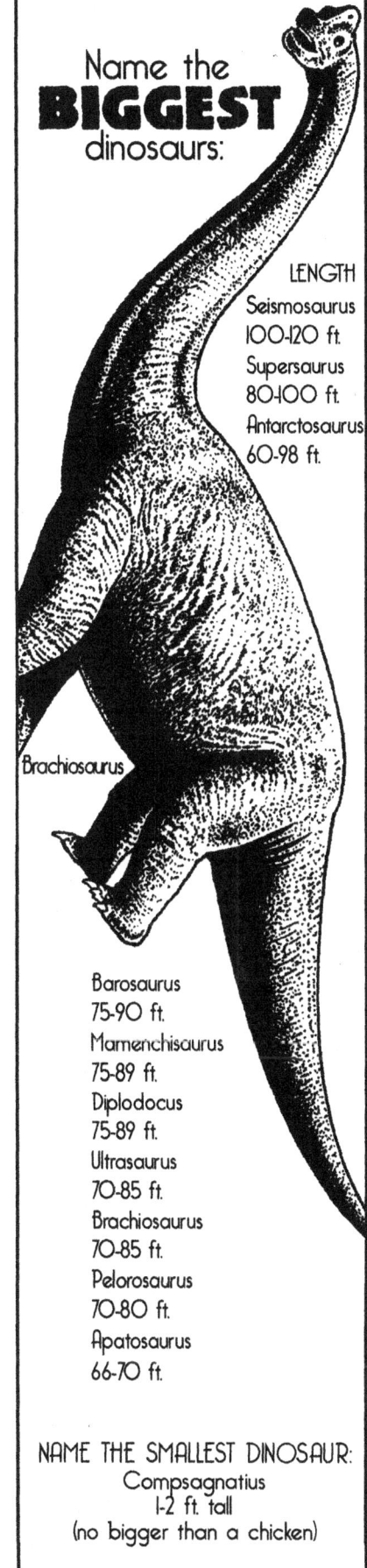

LENGTH
Seismosaurus 100-120 ft.
Supersaurus 80-100 ft.
Antarctosaurus 60-98 ft.

Brachiosaurus

Barosaurus 75-90 ft.
Mamenchisaurus 75-89 ft.
Diplodocus 75-89 ft.
Ultrasaurus 70-85 ft.
Brachiosaurus 70-85 ft.
Pelorosaurus 70-80 ft.
Apatosaurus 66-70 ft.

NAME THE SMALLEST DINOSAUR:
Compsagnatius
1-2 ft. tall
(no bigger than a chicken)

WHEN WAS THE TRIASSIC PERIOD?

DINOSAURS lived during three prehistoric periods.

THE earliest of them was the Triassic Period.

205 to 240 million years ago: The Triassic Period is marked by the early dominance of reptile life and the emergence of gymnosperm plants. The land masses of the earth were just starting to break up. Great, shallow seas washed against the land. It was steamy and warm.

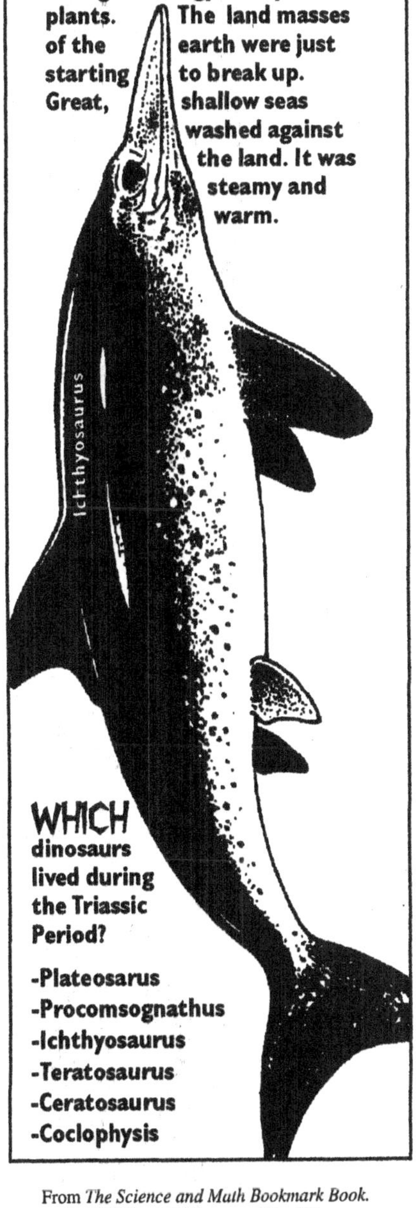

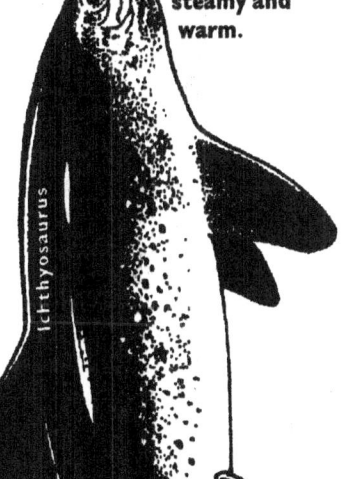

WHICH dinosaurs lived during the Triassic Period?

- Plateosarus
- Procomsognathus
- Ichthyosaurus
- Teratosaurus
- Ceratosaurus
- Coelophysis

WHEN WAS THE JURASSIC PERIOD?

DINOSAURS lived during three prehistoric periods.

THE middle of them was the Jurassic Period.

130 to 205 million years ago: The Jurassic Period marks the height of the dinosaur dominance on Earth. Ferns, palms, rushes and conifers dominate the plant kingdoms. Frogs, lizards, turtles, fish, snails, squid and shark were present. Vast, swampy areas bordered the warm, shallow seas.

WHICH dinosaurs lived during the Triassic Period?

- Aptosaurus
- Brachiosaurus
- Stegasaurus
- Allosaurus
- Diplodocus
- Compsognathus
- Camarasaurus
- Siesmosaurus
- Supersaurus
- Brachiosaurus
- Torosaurus (Dinosaur with the largest head ever recorded for a land animal)

WHEN WAS THE CRETACEOUS PERIOD?

DINOSAURS lived during three prehistoric periods.

THE last of them was the Cretaceous Period.

65 to 138 million years ago: The Cretaceous Period marked the end of the dinosaur dominance on Earth and the emergence of mammals and flowering plants. Modern forest trees emerged: oaks, magnolias and willows. Snakes and birds first appeared. The Cretaceous period ended in a meteor collision with Earth, which wiped out over 70% of all terrestrial species.

WHICH dinosaurs lived during the Cretaceous Period?

- Tyrannosaurus Rex
- Iguanadon 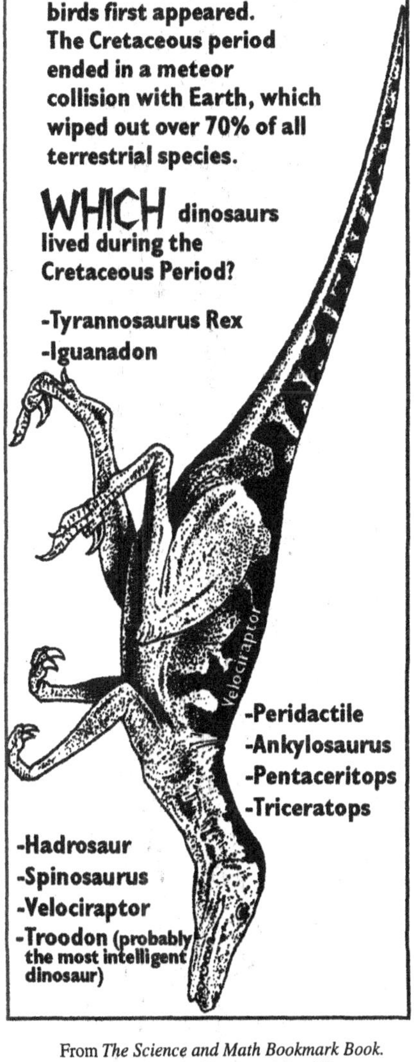
- Peridactile
- Ankylosaurus
- Pentaceritops
- Triceratops
- Hadrosaur
- Spinosaurus
- Velociraptor
- Troodon (probably the most intelligent dinosaur)

WHAT HAS BECOME EXTINCT BESIDES DINOSAURS?

Between 99.8%-99.9% of all plant and animal species that have ever existed are now extinct. Very few modern species are more than one million years old.

What happened to them?

- **EVOLUTION**
  Species are always evolving. Over time, they evolve into new species.

- **MASS EXTINCTION**
  Short periods of mass extinction (like the meteor that killed the dinosaurs) happen periodically.

- **ENVIRONMENTAL CHANGE**
  When essential habitat and food supplies vanish, so do the species that depended on them.

NAME SOME FAMOUS EXTINCT SPECIES: woolly mammoth, sabertooth tiger, dodo, moa, sea cow, European bison. How many more can you name?

IF ONE IS A MOOSE, ARE TWO MISE?

What do we call groups of different animals? See how many you can guess correctly.

1. A **PACK** of _____.
   a. locusts b. wolves c. kangaroos

2. A **SCHOOL** of _____.
   a. parrots b. foxes c. fish

3. A **COLONY** of _____.
   a. termites b. elk c. bears

4. A **POD** of _____.
   a. bees b. whales c. clams

5. A **BRACE** of _____.
   a. ducks b. cattle c. kittens

6. A **FLOCK** of _____.
   a. antelope b. seals c. sheep

7. A **CRUSH** of _____.
   a. rhinoceroses b. hawks c. lions

8. A **KNOT** of _____.
   a. crows b. toads c. snakes

9. A **STRING** of _____.
   a. ponies b. chickens c. monkeys

10. A **BED** of _____.
    a. cats b. birds c. oysters

Ans: 1—b; 2—c; 3—a; 4—b; 5—a; 6—c; 7—a; 8—b; 9—a; 10—c.

Grass Facts

Grass is the largest and most varied family in the plant kingdom. Grasses cover more of the earth's surface than any other vegetation.

Grass grows everywhere—from the frozen tundra to hot tropics, from the arid desert to soggy swamp, from snowy mountain side to cracks in urban sidewalks.

Grasses range from tiny tundra grass less than 1/4 inch tall to towering bamboo from which furniture and fishing poles are made.

Cereal grasses (wheat, oats, barley, rice, etc.) are the basis for the pasta, bread, dinners, and cereal we eat. Hay and alfalfa feed livestock across the world.

More table sugar comes from grass (sugar cane) than from any other source.

You can even make paper from grass.

Close Cousins

What's the difference between:

Butterflies and Moths

Butterflies fly during the day, moths at dusk and night. Butterflies have knobs at the end of their antennae. Butterflies have slender, hairless bodies. Butterflies rest with wings folded up. Moths rest with wings out flat.

Crocodiles and Alligators

Crocodiles are more aggressive and bigger. Alligators rarely exceed 15 feet. Salt water crocs reach 29 feet long. Alligators have broader, less pointed snouts. An alligator's teeth all fit inside the jaw. Several of a croc's teeth stick out on the sides.

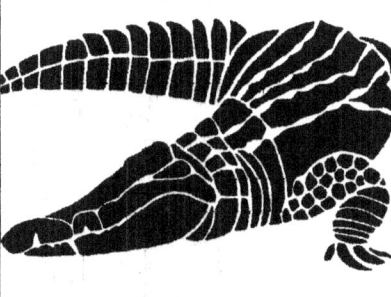

From The Science and Math Bookmark Book.
© 1999 Kendall Haven and Roni Berg.
Teacher Ideas Press. 1-800-237-6124

Close Cousins

What's the difference between:

Grass and Weeds

A weed is any plant that grows where people do not want it to grow. Some plants are considered weeds in one place and not in another. (Morning glories are called weeds in a hay field but can be prized flowers in a garden.) Weeds can be grasses (crab grass or Bermuda grass), vines, flowering plants, annuals, or even shrubs. If no one wants it, it's a weed!

Horse and Zebra

A zebra *is* a horse. It is the only African member of the horse family and the only one that is striped. There are over 30 species of horses alive today. Three of them are zebras.

From The Science and Math Bookmark Book.
© 1999 Kendall Haven and Roni Berg.
Teacher Ideas Press. 1-800-237-6124

Miraculous Transformations

We all know that a caterpillar crawls into a cocoon and emerges as a delicate butterfly. We think it's an amazing transformation. But consider frogs and salmon.

Frogs

hatch as tadpoles. They breathe through gills, absorbing oxygen from water. They have tails and live underwater. In order to become a frog, they have to grow legs and toes, shed their tail, get rid of their gills, grow lungs, and completely reshape their body. They change everything!

Salmon

are hatched in fresh water streams, where they live for several months. Then they swim out into the ocean. It sounds simple, *except*, saltwater and freshwater are so different that salmon have to replace their gills and many of their internal organs in order to swim that last several miles from river to ocean.

From The Science and Math Bookmark Book.
© 1999 Kendall Haven and Roni Berg.
Teacher Ideas Press. 1-800-237-6124

FLOWER AND TREE ANATOMY

Plants have four general parts: roots, trunk, leaves, and flower.

Roots

Roots absorb water and minerals from the soil. Roots also hold the plant upright.

Trunk

(includes branches and stem). The trunk is the transportation system of a plant. Water and minerals are carried up and out to the leaves. Food is carried from the leaves throughout the plant.

Leaves

Leaves absorb carbon dioxide and sunlight. Chlorophyll in the leaves' cells converts these materials into food through photosynthesis. Leaves also expire two waste products into the air: oxygen and water vapor.

Flower

(Includes cones, seeds and nuts.) Flowers are how a plant reproduces.

TREE TRIVIA

Did you know that:

- Photographic film and virtually every building in America has wood in it?
- Two industries: paper/packaging and building account for 90% of our total wood use?
- Recycling paper saves water and energy in addition to trees?
- The average American uses 730 pounds of paper each year. It takes nine trees, each as tall as a four-story building, to produce that much paper.
- Even with all of America's recycling effort, still 40% of our garbage is paper and packaging?
- Many clothes are made from wood. Rayon, Tencel®, acetate, and triacetate are made from pure wood pulp. Do you have any wood clothes in your closet?

WHAT ARE THE PARTS OF AN ECOSYSTEM?

All ecosystems can be divided into three general parts: non-living elements, flora (plants), and fauna (animals). Each of these has several major elements.

Non-Living Elements:

These elements include land and water, the environment, and the climate.

Flora:

Plants include grasses, flowers, shrubs, reeds and vines, moss and lichens, decomposing bacteria, molds and fungus, and trees.

Fauna:

Animals include grazers, browsers, insects, predators, top predators, scavengers, and decomposers.

What is a niche in an ecosystem?

Ecosystems provide food and shelter for every member of the system. If there are grasses, there must be grazers to eat the grass. If there are browsers, there must be leafy trees to feed them. A top predator must have prey species to eat. Scavengers depend on top predators for scraps to eat. The system depends on scavengers and decomposers to clean up the litter. Every member depends on every other member doing their part to support the ecosystem.

Those "parts" are called *niches*. A niche is a specific function within the ecosystem suited for a particular species. A species fills its niche when it is exactly suited for the function it performs. Every member of an ecosystem is a specialist. They specialize in performing their niche.

What is diversity? What does it mean?

A group is diverse if it has lots of different kinds of members.

In the early 1970's, scientists noticed that some new fungi, pollutants and diseases destroyed some ecosystems and did little damage to others. They found that ecosystems with a great variety of kinds of grasses, bushes, trees and animals survived better than those with only a few species in each group.

Because the stable system had more different kinds of members, scientists called them diverse ecosystems. **Diversity became a measure of how strong and resistant to stress an ecosystem is.**

We want ecosystems to be diverse. Scientists worry when plant and animal species die because it reduces diversity.

Is a Forest Fire Good or Bad for a Forest Ecosystem?

Both. Forest fires do great damage, but they also do great good.

Bad: Forest fires destroy plant life. Fires kill many small animals, birds, reptiles, and insects. Fires increase short-term erosion and degrade stream water quality. Fires destroy the habitat for many species.

Good: Forest fires clear away underbrush that chokes out new trees. They enrich the soil with nutrients. They help spread seeds from mature trees. Fires destroy many parasites and diseases of trees. Fires open up the forest to allow needed light into the understory.

While traumatic and catastrophic to the ecosystem, forest fires are occasionally essential to maintain the long-term health of a forest ecosystem.

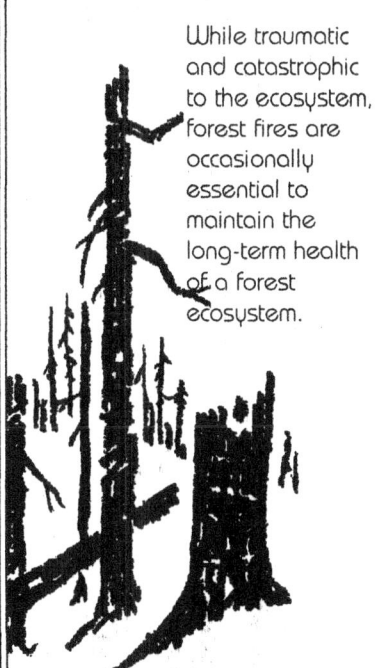

What Happens When One Species In An Ecosystem Is Destroyed?

In diverse ecosystems, there is little effect. But in less diverse systems, or when an entire niche is destroyed, it results in major problems. Until ecosystem concepts were studied, it was hard to anticipate the effects of a change.

Western ranchers hunted wolves to extinction in the early 1900's because they preyed on sheep and cattle. Everyone agreed it would be better for the livestock to be rid of the wolves. But, with no top predator, the wolves' natural prey, mice and rabbits, overpopulated. In a few years grazing fields were swarming with mice and rabbits. They ate all the grasses. Pasture land turned to barren dirt and weeds. Ranchers had to import feed for their livestock. Without adequate grass, grazers died in droves. The animal portion of the ecosystem almost collapsed. In many areas, the ecosystem still hasn't recovered.

In general, when one niche of an ecosystem is removed, the niche it preys on overpopulates and the niche that preys on it starves. Diversity avoids these great swings in a system.

Where does pollution come from?

Pollution comes from all human activity and flows into our air, soil and water. The major categories of pollution are:

AGRICULTURE
Pesticides, fungicides, fertilizers, and manure

LOGGING & LUMBER
Silt, erosion and destroyed forest habitats

INDUSTRIAL ACTIVITY
Heavy metals, hazardous wastes, soot, NOx and SOx, sludge, waste heat, waste water and oil spills

URBAN ACTIVITY
Sewer and storm drain runoff; oils and tars from city runoff; urban spraying to control pests; exhaust from cars, trucks, and lawn mowers; and leakage from land fills

RECREATION
4-wheel drive vehicles, outboard motors, Jet Skis™, trash and engine exhaust

How Much Garbage Do We Create?

Did you know that every **DAY** we Americans toss out:

- 240,000 tons of edible food (9 million cubic feet).
- 125,000 radios and stereos.
- 21,000 video cassette recorders.
- 60,000 TVs.
- 6 million books.
- 800,000 pounds of automobile parts.
- 190,000 tons of boxes, bags and wrappers.
- 79 million greeting cards.
- 600,000 car and truck tires.
- 525 billion gallons of waste water.
- Exhaust from 395 million gallons of burned gasoline.
- 200,000 neck ties.
- Wood shavings from 4 million pencils.
- 15,000 tons of broken plate glass.
- 1 million tons of hazardous waste.
- 57 million disposable diapers.

What's the Endangered Species List?

Congress created the Endangered Species List in 1973 and required that state and federal governments protect and preserve all species on the list.

The list was created to slow the loss of species through extinction from pollution and habitat destruction. Some estimates claim that over 50,000 existing species will be extinct by 2050.

There are now 1135 species of plants and animals listed as endangered. Ten have recovered and have been removed from the list. In mid-1998, an additional 29 species were removed.

What species have been removed? Some of the better-known recovered species include: the bald eagle, peregrine falcon, Aleutian Canada goose, Michigan timber wolf, and the Gulf Coast brown pelican.

FAMOUS SCIENTISTS
DIAN FOSSEY, BIOLOGIST
Studied Gorillas in Africa

Dian Fossey was born in 1932 in San Francisco. She went to college to be a physical therapist, but always wanted to see gorillas in the wild.

In 1966, Louis Leakey helped Fossey start her study of shy gorillas—all alone—in the dense forests of Rwanda, Africa, even though she had no training in biology or in jungle survival. To get close to gorillas, Fossey had to imitate their knuckle walk, their hoots, their grooming practices, and their slapping of chest and thighs.

She discovered that gorillas are shy, smart, kind, gentle, have strong family ties, love to laugh and play, and care for their young and hurt. She wrote *Gorillas in the Mist* about gorillas.

FAMOUS SCIENTISTS
CHARLES DARWIN
Created the Theory of Evolution

Born in England in 1807, Charles Darwin was a naturalist. At 26, he signed on for a four-year voyage aboard the ship HMS *Beagle* to study flora (plants) and fauna (animals) around the world.

Darwin never got over being sea sick and was sick every day for all four years at sea.

During that voyage he created the theory of evolution. At the isolated Galapagos Islands in the Pacific Ocean, he found that the beaks of finches were different on each island and had specialized to be perfectly suited for the available food supply on that island. He realized that, over time, the birds had **evolved** to suit their environment. Over time, he realized that all species evolve to suit their environment.

FAMOUS SCIENTISTS

LOUIS PASTEUR, BIOLOGIST
Discovered the Existence of Germs

Louis Pasteur was born in France in 1820. He was Vice President of a famous Paris university.

For thousands of years people believed that living organisms spontaneously materialized from non-living matter—that rats materialized from old rags and cheese, eels from mud, worms from rotting meat, and yeast materialized from grain to ferment beer and wine.

In 1858, Pasteur conducted experiments that proved that microscopic bacteria (germs) floated invisibly in the air and simply landed on rotting meat and bread, and that they would not grow in a sterile environment.

The theory of sterilization of medical equipment and food preparation areas came out of Pasteur's work. The pasteurization process to remove germs and bacteria from milk is named for him.

FAMOUS SCIENTISTS

GREGOR MENDEL
Discovered how Heredity Works

Austrian monk Gregor Mendel grew peas in the 1860's—not to eat, but to study heredity, or how physical traits are passed from generation to generation.

He mixed tall pea plants with short ones. The second generation plants were *all* tall. In the third generation he got one short plant for every three tall ones. He mixed yellow peas with green peas and got all yellow peas. In the third generation he got one green pea for every three yellow peas. The traits never mixed.

Gregor Mendel discovered the laws of heredity that work for all species: each parent gives one trait to each new plant. One trait is dominant (e.g.: being tall) and appears whenever it is present. The other is recessive (being short) and only appears when the dominant trait is absent.

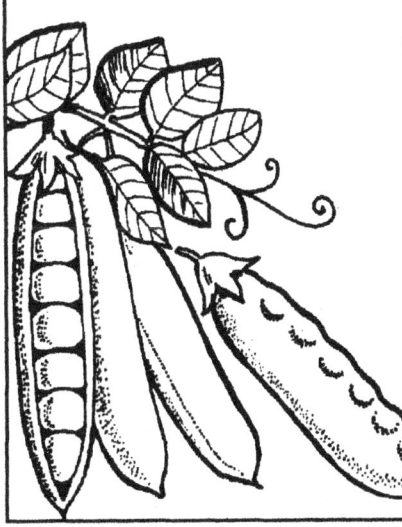

FAMOUS SCIENTISTS

JANE GOODALL
Studied Chimpanzees

Born in England in 1934, Jane Goodall was a secretary and had never taken a biology course when she met famed anthropologist Louis Leakey. She had, however, always loved animals. Her first stuffed doll had been a baby chimpanzee.

Leakey wanted to send her into the African forests at the age of 24 to study chimps because very little was known about them. Such animal studies in the wild were too dangerous and too hard to control and so were rarely conducted.

Jane Goodall went alone into Africa to study chimps—and stayed for 34 years! Most of what we know about chimps we owe to Goodall.

Jane Goodall has written several books of her adventures and now fights to protect the safety and rights of animals caged in zoos.

Math

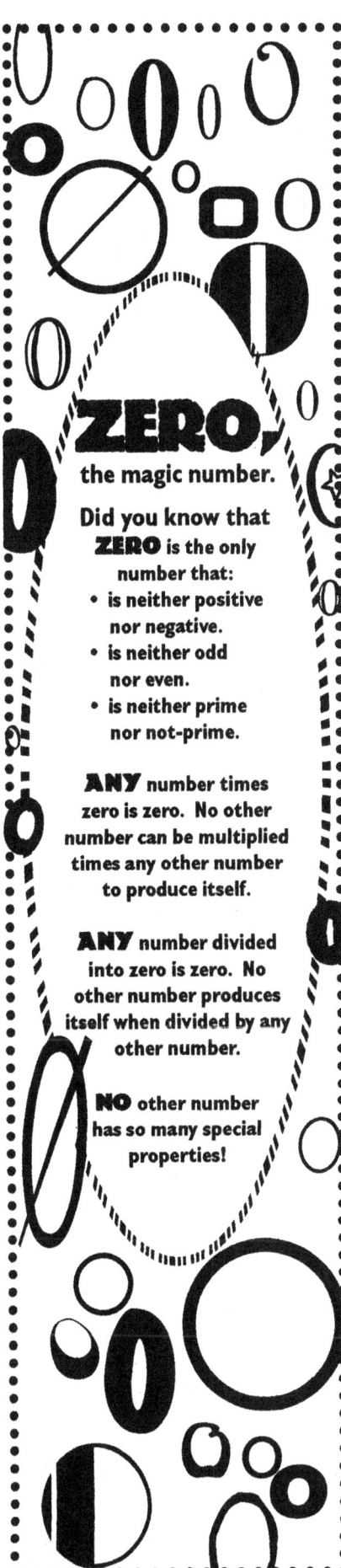

ZERO, the magic number.

Did you know that **ZERO** is the only number that:
- is neither positive nor negative.
- is neither odd nor even.
- is neither prime nor not-prime.

ANY number times zero is zero. No other number can be multiplied times any other number to produce itself.

ANY number divided into zero is zero. No other number produces itself when divided by any other number.

NO other number has so many special properties!

From *The Science and Math Bookmark Book*.
© 1999 Kendall Haven and Roni Berg.
Teacher Ideas Press. 1-800-237-6124

Can you name the seven different parts of our number system?

Whole **N**umbers
(1, 2, 3...) often called integers

Negative **N**umbers
(-1, -2, -3...)

Fractions
(1/2, 1/3, 1/4...)

Zero
(a special number connecting positive and negative)

Irrational **N**umbers
($\sqrt{2}$, $\sqrt{3}$, π...)

Imaginary **N**umbers
(1i, 2i, 3i...)

Surreal **N**umbers
($\infty+1$, $\infty+2$...)

Few people use imaginary and surreal numbers. But we all use the other five in the course of our daily lives.

From *The Science and Math Bookmark Book*.
© 1999 Kendall Haven and Roni Berg.
Teacher Ideas Press. 1-800-237-6124

Why were all the different kinds of numbers developed?

People needed to count, add and multiply, so they invented *whole numbers*.

They needed to subtract, so they invented *negative numbers*, so they could subtract 9 from 4.

They needed to divide, so they invented *fractions*.

They needed a continuous number system, so they invented *zero* to connect positive and negative, so they could subtract 8 from 8.

They found there were numbers they couldn't express as simple fractions, so they invented *irrational numbers*.

Mathematicians couldn't solve problems that involved the square root of a negative number, so they invented *imaginary numbers*.

Mathematicians found a need to count beyond infinity, so they invented *surreal numbers*.

From *The Science and Math Bookmark Book*.
© 1999 Kendall Haven and Roni Berg.
Teacher Ideas Press. 1-800-237-6124

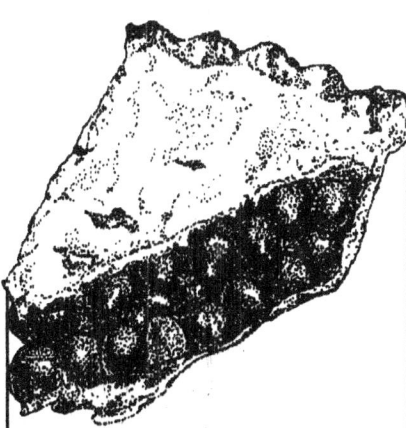

WHAT IS PI (π)? WHAT'S SO SPECIAL ABOUT IT?

- π is found by dividing the circumference of a circle (distance around the circle) by its diameter (the distance across the circle). That ratio is exactly the same for every circle! It is a constant we call *pi*, or π.

- Most people use 3.14 for π. But it is really equal to 3.1415926535 897932384626433..... and so on forever! π is not an even fraction, so its exact value can never be determined. We always have to round off somewhere.

- Circles are special and useful shapes, but their size, area, and circumference are hard to measure because they are round. Pi (π) is a special number that helps us measure the area of circles and the volume of spheres (balls).

From *The Science and Math Bookmark Book*.
© 1999 Kendall Haven and Roni Berg.
Teacher Ideas Press. 1-800-237-6124

What is a prime number? How many are there?

Prime numbers are a special group of numbers.

They are numbers that cannot be divided evenly by any number except for themselves and one.

Mathematicians have always thought prime numbers are important and special and have studied their properties and patterns.

How many prime numbers can you find?

In the lunch box above are the first prime numbers (but one number is missing). Can you tell which number it is?

Answer: 17

From *The Science and Math Bookmark Book*.
© 1999 Kendall Haven and Roni Berg.
Teacher Ideas Press. 1-800-237-6124

We use a base-ten number system. Computers use a base-two system. (All the information they store is in the form of either a 1 or a 0.) The base number tells you how many single digit numbers there are. (More precisely, it tells you when you come to the first two-digit number. In a base-10 system, the first two-digit number is the tenth number in the system.) You can count using a system with any base number.

Base 10	Base 2	Base 5	Base 12
1	1	1	1
2	10	2	2
3	11	3	3
4	100	4	4
5	101	10	5
6	110	11	6
7	111	12	7
8	1000	13	8
9	1001	14	9
10	1010	20	*
11	1011	21	#
12	1100	22	10

What would our number 24 be in a base three system?

Ans: 220

From *The Science and Math Bookmark Book*.
© 1999 Kendall Haven and Roni Berg.
Teacher Ideas Press. 1-800-237-6124

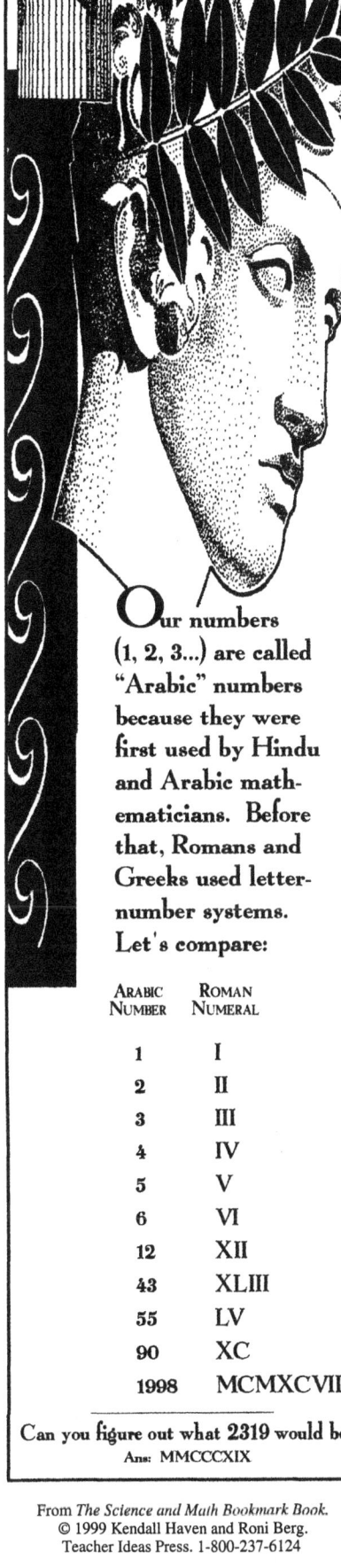

The Name of Our Numbers:

Our numbers (1, 2, 3...) are called "Arabic" numbers because they were first used by Hindu and Arabic mathematicians. Before that, Romans and Greeks used letter-number systems. Let's compare:

Arabic Number	Roman Numeral
1	I
2	II
3	III
4	IV
5	V
6	VI
12	XII
43	XLIII
55	LV
90	XC
1998	MCMXCVIII

Can you figure out what 2319 would be?
Ans: MMCCCXIX

From *The Science and Math Bookmark Book*.
© 1999 Kendall Haven and Roni Berg.
Teacher Ideas Press. 1-800-237-6124

NAME THAT FRACTION!

Fractions are ratios of whole numbers. Fractions are created when one number is divided into another. Can you draw a line connecting each fraction with its decimal equivalent?

FRACTION	DECIMAL
1/3 — Example	0.500
1/4	0.667
1/6	0.333
2/3	0.750
3/8	0.250
5/6	0.167
4/8	0.375
3/4	0.833

Ans: 1/3—.333; 1/4—.250; 1/6—.167; 2/3—.677; 3/8—.375; 5/6—.833; 4/8—.500; 3/4—.750.

BONUS QUESTION: Which one of the fractions above is improperly written?

Ans: 4/8. It should be reduced to its simpler form, 1/2.

From *The Science and Math Bookmark Book*.
© 1999 Kendall Haven and Roni Berg.
Teacher Ideas Press. 1-800-237-6124

WHAT IS INFINITY?

Infinity isn't really a number. Rather, it means "beyond all known numbers."

What is the symbol for infinity? ∞ (It looks like a sideways eight.)

What's different about infinity? Infinity has many unique properties because it isn't a specific number, but rather it represents a whole region of numbers.

$$\infty + 1 = \infty \,!$$
$$\infty + \infty = \infty \,!!$$
$$\infty \div 2 = \infty \,!!!$$

Anything you do to

∞

still equals infinity.

That's very different from every other number.

From *The Science and Math Bookmark Book*.
© 1999 Kendall Haven and Roni Berg.
Teacher Ideas Press. 1-800-237-6124

What is the World's Oldest Known Math Puzzle?

It dates from an Egyptian scroll dated 1,650 BC.

This puzzle is 3,650 years old and we still use it today!

From the scroll it reads:

"As I was walking to St. Ives, I met a man with seven wives. Every wife had seven sacks. Every sack had seven cats. Every cat had seven kits. Kits, cats, sacks, wives, how many were going to St. Ives?"

Answer: Just 1.

Perfect Numbers

Do you know what they are?

Ancient mathematicians studied numbers very carefully. They especially liked to *factor* numbers.

Factors are smaller numbers which, when multiplied together, make the original number. The factors of 12 could either be 1, 3 and 4 (1 X 3 X 4 = 12) or 1, 2 and 6 (1 X 2 X 6 = 12).

Mathematicians noticed that if they added together all of the possible factors of a number, sometimes that sum equaled the original number. They called these numbers perfect numbers and thought they had magical powers.

Two perfect numbers are: 6 (1+2+3) and 28 (14+2+7+4+1). Can you find any others?

"X" Marks The Spot

ALGEBRA USES EQUATIONS TO SOLVE PROBLEMS. WHAT IS AN EQUATION?

An equation says that two amounts are equal, but says it in math terms instead of in a written-out sentence. An equal sign (=) separates the two amounts that are equal. It shows that two amounts are equal.

Equations are used when we don't know the value of one of the numbers. We put a letter into the equation to represent the number we don't know. We usually use "X" for the unknown number.

X + 3 = 7 is an equation with one unknown number. It says that some amount, "X", added to 3 equals 7. We then use arithmetic functions to find out what the unknown number is. This process is called *solving the equation*.

We know that 4 + 3 = 7 so "X" in this equation must equal 4.

Math 98

ALGEBRAIC SYMBOLS YOU SHOULD KNOW

Match each symbol with its written description.

−	**S**ubtract
±	**E**ither add or subtract
=	**I**s equal to
≥	**I**s either greater than or equal to
≈	**I**s approximately equal to
√	**T**ake the square root of
÷	**D**ivide by
≠	**I**s not equal to
+	**A**dd
<	**I**s less than
≤	**I**s either less than or equal to
>	**I**s greater than

ANS: = is equal to; > is greater than; < is less than; − subtract; + add; ± either add or subtract; ≠ is not equal to; ≥ is either greater than or equal to; ≤ is either less than or equal to; √ take the square root of; ≈ is approximately equal to; ÷ divide by.

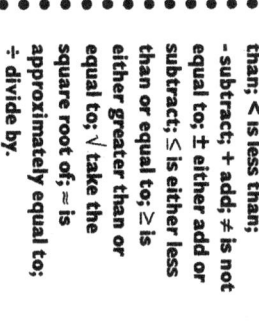

From *The Science and Math Bookmark Book.*
© 1999 Kendall Haven and Roni Berg.
Teacher Ideas Press. 1-800-237-6124

Can you make a magic square?

A magic square is one in which the sum of the numbers you write into each box in each row, in each column, and along the diagonals add to the same total. No number may be used more than once.

Using the numbers 1 through 9, make a magic square in the boxes below.

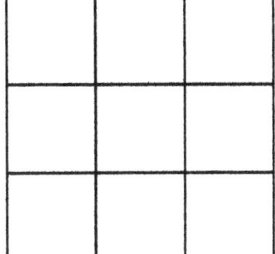

There are many ways to arrange the numbers. Here is a typical solution: top row: 4, 3, 8; middle row: 9, 5, 1; bottom row: 2, 7, 6.

BONUS QUESTION: Can you make a 9-box magic square without using 5 in the middle square?

Ans: No.

From *The Science and Math Bookmark Book.*
© 1999 Kendall Haven and Roni Berg.
Teacher Ideas Press. 1-800-237-6124

Identify these two-dimensional regular shapes:

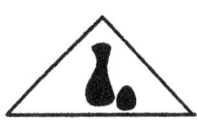
1.

2.

3.

4.

5.

(**Ans:** 1.–triangle, 2.–rectangle, 3.–pentagon, 4.–hexagon, 5.–octagon.)

Bonus Question: What are the names of a seven-sided and a nine-sided regular shape?

Ans: heptagon and nonagon.

From *The Science and Math Bookmark Book.*
© 1999 Kendall Haven and Roni Berg.
Teacher Ideas Press. 1-800-237-6124

Can you name each of the four-sided shapes below? Do you know the difference between each of the shapes?

1.
2.
3.
4.
5.

Answer

1. —SQUARE. All sides and angles are equal.
2. —RECTANGLE. All angles are equal, but the sides are not.
3. —PARALLELOGRAM. Each pair of opposite sides is parallel and the same length but angles are not all equal.
4. —TRAPEZOID. The base and top are parallel but not the same length. The sides may or may not be the same length.
5. —QUADRILATERAL. None of the sides or angles are equal.

From *The Science and Math Bookmark Book.*
© 1999 Kendall Haven and Roni Berg.
Teacher Ideas Press. 1-800-237-6124

Getting The Angle On Triangles

There are two ways to group triangles: either by comparing the three angles in the triangle, or by comparing the three sides.

Scalene Triangles
have no sides equal and no equal angles.

A. Scalene obtuse triangles have one angle greater than 90°.

B. In scalene acute triangles, all angles are less than 90°.

Isosceles Triangles
have two sides of the same length, thus they also have two equal angles.

Right Triangles
have one 90° angle. They may either be scalene acute (**A.**) or isosceles (**B.**). The 90° angle, called a right angle or perpendicular angle, gives the triangle many special properties.

Equilateral Triangles
have all three sides of equal length. All three angles in equilateral triangles are also automatically equal.

From *The Science and Math Bookmark Book.*
© 1999 Kendall Haven and Roni Berg.
Teacher Ideas Press. 1-800-237-6124

There are four regular curved shapes: CIRCLE, ELLIPSE, PARABOLA and HYPERBOLA.

Can you identify each below?

These curved shapes are called "conic sections" because they are made by slicing at different angles through a cone.

1.
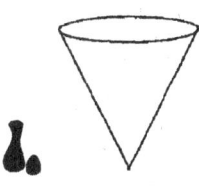

2.
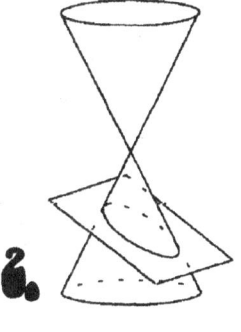

3.
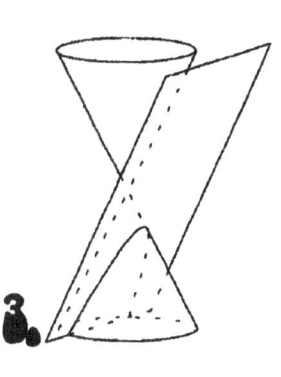

4.
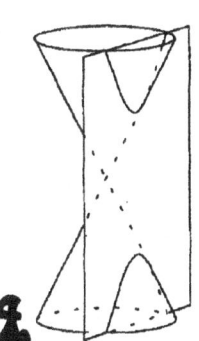

(Ans: 1.—circle. 2.—ellipse. 3.—parabola. 4.—hyperbola.)

From *The Science and Math Bookmark Book.*
© 1999 Kendall Haven and Roni Berg.
Teacher Ideas Press. 1-800-237-6124

How many measures of volume do you know?

1 acre-foot = 43,560 cubic feet

1 cubic foot = 1728 cubic inches

1 bushel = 4 pecks

1 peck = 2 gallons

1 gallon = 4 quarts

1 quart = 2 pints

1 pint = 2 cups

1 cup = 8 fluid ounces

1 fluid ounce = 2 tablespoons

1 tablespoon = 3 teaspoons

1 teaspoon = 3/4 of a fluid dram

1 fluid dram = 60 minims

There are 276,480 minims in a bushel.... Tell that to your grocer!

From *The Science and Math Bookmark Book.*
© 1999 Kendall Haven and Roni Berg.
Teacher Ideas Press. 1-800-237-6124

WHAT IS ALGEBRA? WHAT IS ARITHMETIC?

Algebra is one part of math. Algebra uses arithmetic processes to search for the value of unknown quantities.

The name "algebra" comes from an Arabic word, *al-jabra*, which means "the solution."

Arithmetic is simply the manipulation of numbers by addition, subtraction, multiplication and division.

Arithmetic is what we use in algebra. Algebra <u>solves</u> problems.

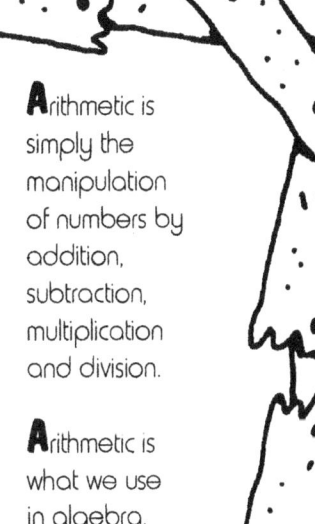

From *The Science and Math Bookmark Book.*
© 1999 Kendall Haven and Roni Berg.
Teacher Ideas Press. 1-800-237-6124

How to...

...find the area of a rectangle:
Area equals the height times the width—
$A = wh$

...find the area of a circle:
Area equals the number pi times the radius times the radius again—
$A = \pi r^2$

...find the area of a triangle:
Area equals one half of the base times the height—
$A = 1/2\, wh$

From *The Science and Math Bookmark Book.*
© 1999 Kendall Haven and Roni Berg.
Teacher Ideas Press. 1-800-237-6124

How to find the volume...

of a sphere:
Volume equals 1/3 of the number pi times the radius, times the radius again, and times the radius again—
$V = 1/3 \pi r^3$

of a cube:
Volume equals the length of one side times itself and times itself again—
$V = w^3$

of a pyramid:
Volume equals 1/3 of the width and length of the base times the height—
$V = 1/3 wbh$

of a cone:
Volume equals 1/3 of the number pi times the radius, times the radius again, times the height—
$V = 1/3 \pi r^2 h$

of a cylinder:
volume equals the number pi times the radius, times the radius again, times the height—
$V = \pi r^2 h$

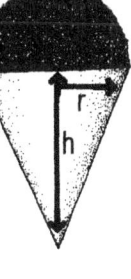

From *The Science and Math Bookmark Book.*
© 1999 Kendall Haven and Roni Berg.
Teacher Ideas Press. 1-800-237-6124

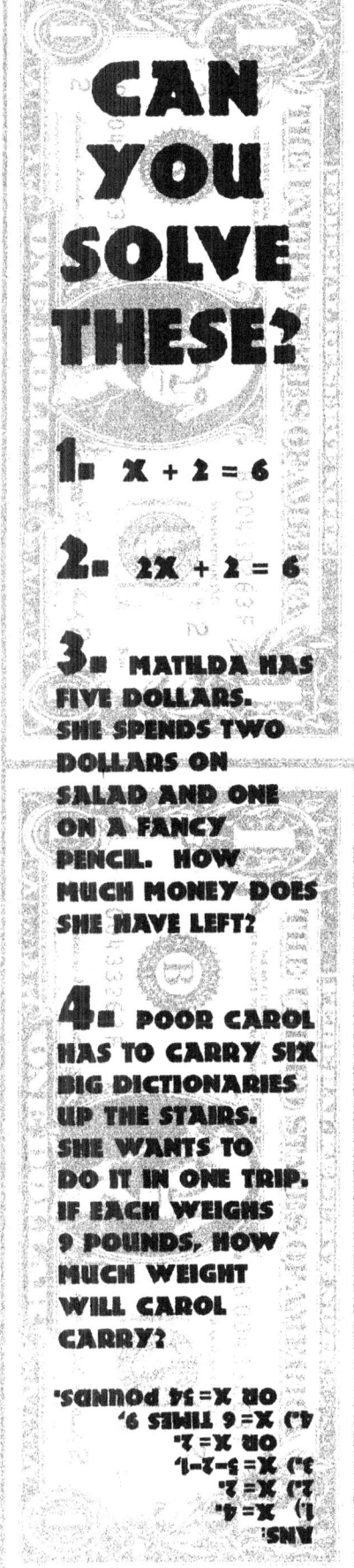

CAN YOU SOLVE THESE?

1. $x + 2 = 6$

2. $2x + 2 = 6$

3. MATILDA HAS FIVE DOLLARS. SHE SPENDS TWO DOLLARS ON SALAD AND ONE ON A FANCY PENCIL. HOW MUCH MONEY DOES SHE HAVE LEFT?

4. POOR CAROL HAS TO CARRY SIX BIG DICTIONARIES UP THE STAIRS. SHE WANTS TO DO IT IN ONE TRIP. IF EACH WEIGHS 9 POUNDS, HOW MUCH WEIGHT WILL CAROL CARRY?

ANS:
1.) X = 4.
2.) X = 2.
3.) X = 5−2−1, OR X = 2.
4.) X = 6 TIMES 9, OR X = 54 POUNDS.

From *The Science and Math Bookmark Book.*
© 1999 Kendall Haven and Roni Berg.
Teacher Ideas Press. 1-800-237-6124

The world's first computer was designed by Charles Babbage in 1822. He designed it, but couldn't build it. No one could manufacture the parts he needed.

The first computer was built in Cambridge, MA, by Howard Aiken in 1944. It was called the Mark I, stood 51 feet long by 8 feet high, and made 12 calculations per second. A small laptop now can make over two million calculations per second.

Computers had no memory until An Wang invented memory cores in 1949.

The first calculator, also invented by An Wang, was built in 1963.

The first word processor wasn't built until 1975 (also invented by An Wang).

The first personal computer wasn't built until 1977.

From *The Science and Math Bookmark Book.*
© 1999 Kendall Haven and Roni Berg.
Teacher Ideas Press. 1-800-237-6124

LET'S COMPARE METRIC AND U.S. MEASUREMENTS

Length
CENTIMETER: 2.54 centimeters = 1"
METER: 1 meter = 39.36"
KILOMETER: 1 kilometer = 0.62 miles

Mass
GRAM: 28.3 grams = 1 ounce
KILOGRAM: 1 kilogram = 2.2 pounds

Volume
LITER: 1 liter = 0.88 quarts
LITER: 1 liter = 3.52 cups

Speed
METER per second:
1 mps = 3.28 feet per second
KILOMETERS per hour:
1 kph = 0.62 mph
80 kph = 55 mph

Area
SQUARE METERS:
1 sq. meter = 10.76 sq. feet
SQUARE KILOMETER:

 But we all use the same time:
60 seconds in a minute;
60 minutes in an hour;
24 hours in a day.

FAMOUS MATHEMATICIANS

ARCHIMEDES
Invented Levers, Corkscrew Water Pumps, the Catapult, and Discovered Buoyancy and the Formula for the Volume of a Sphere

Archimedes was born on the Mediterranean island of Sicily in 286 BC. He was called the greatest thinker and mathematician of all time. He would draw figures on the dirt floor of his house and think about a problem for days on end.

Twice he saved Sicily from invading Roman armies with his inventions. When the king thought a gold smith had cheated him (232 BC), Archimedes discovered the principle of buoyancy. While watching boys play with driftwood on the beach (258 BC) he discovered the principle of the lever. Archimedes thought his greatest achievement was discovering the formula for the volume of a sphere.

FAMOUS MATHEMATICIANS

ISAAC NEWTON
Invented Calculus, Discovered Gravity, and Created the Laws of Motion

Isaac Newton was a frail young man of 21 when the terrible plague closed English universities and forced professors to scatter into the countryside where it was safe.

There Newton wondered a lot about the moon. Why didn't it fall to Earth? Why didn't the Earth fall toward the sun? He discovered that all movement (motion) is caused by forces. Some force must act (push or pull on an object) to create or change a motion.

He discovered the force of gravity and his three laws of motion, which became the basis for all physics over the next 250 years. He also created calculus as a way to solve mathematics problems algebra could not handle...all before he was 25 years old!

FAMOUS MATHEMATICIANS

PIERRE DE FERMAT
Discovered the Laws of Probability

If you flip a coin, what are the odds it will land heads-up? If you flip it twice, what are the odds *both* flips will land heads-up? Roll a pair of dice. What are the odds you'll roll a seven? That's probability.

Pierre de Fermat discovered the laws of probability in 1654. Pierre was a lawyer and amateur mathematician. While watching a court case, he wondered which lawyer was winning. He realized he needed to count the number of points each lawyer still needed to make in order to sway the judge.

It started him thinking about gambling games men played with dice. Probability was born! We use it every day to predict the weather, the stock market, the economy, and the likelihood of passing a test!

From *The Science and Math Bookmark Book*.
© 1999 Kendall Haven and Roni Berg.
Teacher Ideas Press. 1-800-237-6124

FAMOUS MATHEMATICIANS
EUCLID
Created Euclidean Geometry and Deductive Reasoning

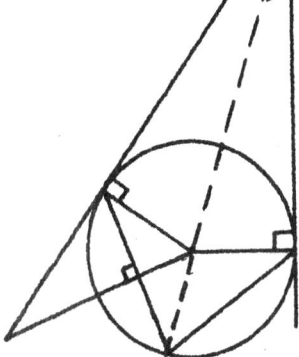

In 315 BC, King Ptolomy of Alexandria, Egypt, created the Alexandria Museum (university) and library. It was the greatest collection of knowledge ever assembled—over 600,000 scrolls, over 20,000 statues, over 30,000 pieces of art.

King Ptolomy sought the Greek mathematician, Euclid, to head the Museum's math department. Euclid taught and wrote. Euclid's greatest work, called **The Elements**, was a 13-volume book that contained all known math and geometry.

Euclid's **Elements** created the field of geometry, provided over 450 math theorems and proofs, and created the process of logical, deductive reasoning.

2,500 years later, we still use Euclid's theorems and teachings; we still call geometry "Euclidean Geometry."

From *The Science and Math Bookmark Book*.
© 1999 Kendall Haven and Roni Berg.
Teacher Ideas Press. 1-800-237-6124

FAMOUS MATHEMATICIANS
SOPHIE GERMAIN
First Woman Awarded a Mathematics Degree

Sophie was born in Paris in 1776. She loved mathematics.

But Sophie's parents believed that study would make a girl sick, that too much thinking would ruin her health.

So Sophie secretly studied in her room at night. She borrowed notes from a neighbor boy.

In 1794, Sophie wrote a math paper. Her friend turned it in with his paper. Sophie's paper won the contest for the best math paper at the university. All the professors were shocked! So were Sophie's parents.

Sophie Germain became France's best mathematician. She helped design the Eiffel Tower and was the first woman to receive a math degree in all of Europe. In 1816, Napoleon awarded her the Grand Prize of the French Academy of Sciences.

From *The Science and Math Bookmark Book*.
© 1999 Kendall Haven and Roni Berg.
Teacher Ideas Press. 1-800-237-6124

FAMOUS MATHEMATICIANS

SONYA KOVALEVSKY
First Woman Mathematics Professor

Sonya was born in Russia in 1838. There were no math jobs for women, no scholarships, no professorships. Universities wouldn't admit women students. In Russia they believed that math was unladylike and girls who studied should be punished.

But Sonya loved mathematics. In 1860, the University of Berlin allowed women to study. Sonya enrolled. However, the university refused to grant a degree to a woman.

Sonya wrote five papers so brilliant, they became part of the University's math classes. Then the University *had* to give her a degree. But they still wouldn't hire her to teach.

In 1887, the University of Stockholm offered her a professorship. She became the most famous woman in Sweden. Sonya became the most popular name for Swedish girls.

FAMOUS MATHEMATICIANS

JOHN NAPIER
Invented Logarithms and the World's First Calculator

John Napier was a Scottish nobleman born in 1550. He didn't think of himself as a mathematician. He just wanted to solve everyday problems. Mostly, he wanted to find ways to grow more oats in his wide fields.

He invented logarithms to make it easier and faster to multiply big numbers.

He also created the world's first calculator to make multiplication fast. Superstitious townsfolk thought Napier was a wizard because of all his experimenting and because of the mathematics he invented. They called Napier's calculator "Napier's Bones" because a rumor said he made the ivory strips used in his calculator out of bones during magical ceremonies in his castle tower.

FAMOUS MATHEMATICIANS

AL KHWARIZMI
Discovered that Zero was Actually a Number

Neither Greeks, Romans, nor Hebrews had a number for zero. Euclid never thought of creating a number for zero. Neither did Archimedes or Plato.

Hindu mathematicians in southern India first created zero. But it wasn't a number to them. It was just a place holder for where there was no number. They called it "sifr," meaning "an empty place."

In 800 AD, Arabic mathematician Al Khwarizmi in Baghdad realized that zero had to be a number to make division and subtraction possible. Al Khwarizmi talked the caliph (king) into declaring that zero was a number.

Al Khwarizmi named it "zero."

Al Khwarizmi also created the name "algebra" from the Arabic "al jabra" meaning "the solution."

Index

A

Abell 2020, 7
Abominable snowman, 69
Acceleration, 19
Acid rain, 74
Acids, 11, 12
Adriatic Sea, 53
Aegean Sea, 53
Africa, 58
Agriculture
    pollution from, 90
Aiken, Howard, 33, 101
Air, 49, 50
Air conditioning, 33
Airplanes, 27, 33
Al Khwarizmi, 104
Alaska, 39, 42
Alaskan King crabs, 62
Alchemy, 35
Aleutian Island chain, 39
Alexandria Museum and Library (Egypt), 103
Algae, 69
Algebra, 97, 98, 100
Alkaline battery, 33
Allergies, 82
Alligators, 87
Alpha Centauri, 10
Alpha Orions, 7
Amazon River (South America), 38
Amphibians, 67, 68
Anaconda snake, 71
Angel Falls (Venezuela), 38
Animal kingdom, 66, 67
Animals, 66
    biggest on Earth, 71
    fastest, 72
    names for groups of, 86
    numbers of kinds of, 68
    in space, 9
Antarctic currents, 60
Antarctic Ocean, 53
Antarctica, 58
    glaciers in, 45
Antarctosaurus, 84
Anthropology, 66
Antibodies, 82
Apatosaurus, 84
Appalachian Mountain Range, 43
Appert, Nicolas, 32

Arabian Sea, 44, 53
Arabic numbers, 96
Archimedes, 102, 104
Arctic Ocean, 44
Area, 100, 102
Argon, 48
Arithmetic, 100
Armadillo, 73
Armored tank, 33
Arteries, 74, 75
Arthritis, 82
Artificial electricity, 16
Asia, 58
Aspdin, Joseph, 32
Astatine, 11
Asteroids, 5
Astronomers, 10, 25
Astronomical units, 10
Astronomy, 2
Atlantic Ocean, 44, 53, 56
Atmosphere, 48, 51, 63
Atoms, 13, 14, 15, 29
Australia, 58
    in space, 9
Automobiles, 31
Avalanche, 45
Azimuth
    of star, 28

B

Babbage, Charles, 101
Bacon, Roger, 35
Bacteria, 67, 82
Baffin Island, 43
Bain, Alexander, 32
Baltic Sea, 53
Banana trees, 71
Banyan trees, 71
Barnacle, 63
Barnard's Star, 10
Barosaurus, 84
Baseballs, 27
Bases, 11, 12
Base-ten number system, 95
Base-two number system, 95
Battery, 32
Bay, 53, 62
Bay of Fundy (Canada), 56

Bayou, 58
B-cells, 82
Beaches, 54
Beaufort scale, 64
Beetles, 72
Bell, Alexander Graham, 33
Benesch, Alfred, 33
Benz, Carl, 31
Bering Sea, 44, 53
Bering Strait, 39
Bernoulli, Daniel, 27
Bertouli, Nicoli, 32
Bicycle, 32
Bier, Norman, 33
Bifocal glasses, 32
Big Bang, 6
Big Dipper constellation, 28
Big Foot, 69
Binoculars, 33
Biology, 66
Birds, 67, 68, 72
Birdseye, Clarence, 33
Black cherry tree, 70
Black hole, 8, 9
Black Sea, 53
Blood, 75
Blood transfusion, 83
Blue whales, 71, 74
Bluefin tuna, 72
Bone marrow, 75
Borneo, 43
Bostel, David, 33
Box elder tree, 70
Brachiosaurus, 84
Brain, 76, 77
Brearley, Harry, 33
British Thermal Units (BTUs), 26
Brook, 58
Brook Mountain Range, 43
Brown hare, 72
Budding, Edwin, 32
Buoyancy, principle of, 102
Bush, 67
Bushnell, David, 32
Bushnell, Nolan, 33
Butterflies, 87

C

Cainman, C., 33
Calculators, 104
Calculus, 102
California, 42
Calories, 26
Camera, 32
Candy bar, 33
Canine teeth, 84
Canned food, 32
Cape Blanco, Oregon, 39
Capillaries, 74, 75
Car radio, 33
Carbohydrates, 82
Carbon, 12, 50
Carbon chains, 23
Carbon dating, 48
Caribbean Sea, 44, 53
Carlsbad Caverns, New Mexico, 39
Carnivores, 71
Carothers, Wallace, 33
Carrier, Willis, 33
Cars, 31
Cartilage, 83
Carver, Washington, 33
Cascade Mountain Range, 43
Caspian Sea, 53
Cats, 73
Catskill Mountain Range, 43
Caverns, 39
Caves, 41
Cells, 78, 79
Cement, 32
Cenozoic era, 47
Centaur, 69
Centigrade scale, 14, 26
Century, 23
Cereal, breakfast, 33
Ceres, 5
CFCs (Chlorofluorocarbons), 63
Charlton, John, 33
Cheetahs, 72
Chemical electricity, 15
Chemistry, 2, 23
Chicagof (Alaska), 43
Chimpanzees, 92
China
    first recorded use of rocket in, 32
Chlorine, 28
Chlorine bleach, 32
Chlorofluorocarbons (CFCs), 63
Chocolate milk, 33
Circles, 95, 99
Circulatory system, 74, 75
Cirrhosis, 80
Cirus clouds, 49
Civil War (American)
    rockets used in, 32
Clams, 63
Class, 68
Clouds, 49, 58

Coastal zone, 54
Coldest places
    in U.S., 44
Color TV, 33
Colorado Desert, 60
Comets, 6, 28
Compounds, 9
Compsagnatius, 84
Computers, 33, 95, 101
Cones
    volume of, 101
Congreve, William, 32
Conic sections, 99
Constellations, 28
Contact lens, 33
"Contiguous" 48 states, 39
Continents, 58
Copernicus, Nicholas, 34
Copier, 33
Copper, 28
Coral Sea, 53
Corals, 73
Cotton gin, 32
Cottonwood tree, 70
Cousteau, Jacques, 54
Crabs, 62
Creek, 58
Cretaceous period, 47, 85
Crick, Francis, 81
Crickets, 78
Crocodiles, 87
Crooks, Edward, 36
Crossword puzzle, 33
Crustaceans, 62, 67, 68
Cubes
    volume of, 101
Cugnot, Nicolas, 31
Cumulus clouds, 49
Curie, Marie, 35
Currents
    electric, 16
    ocean, 60
Curved shapes, 99
Cyclones, 45, 64
Cylinders
    volume of, 101

D

Dams, 30
Danakil (Ethiopia), 41
Darwin, Charles, 32, 69, 91
Darz, Humphrey, 32
Davis, Francis, 31
Day, 23

Dead Sea, 41, 53
Death Valley (California), 41, 44, 60
Decade, 23
Decimals, 96
De Fermat, Pierre, 103
Deep bottom currents, 60
Deluge, 57
Deoxyribonucleic acid (DNA), 23, 79, 81
Dental drill, 32
Deserts, 60
Dew, 57
Dew point, 50
Diamond, 11
Digestive system, 80
Dinoflagellates, 61
Dinosaurs, 47, 84, 85
Diplodocus, 84
Dirt, 59
Diversity, 89, 90
DNA (deoxyribonucleic acid), 23, 79, 81
Dolphin, 62
Dominant traits (heredity), 92
Douglas fir trees, 70
Dragon, 69
Drake, Edward, 33
Dreams, 81
Drem, Richard, 33
Drizzle, 57
Drought, 45
Dust devils, 63
Dust storm, 45

E

Ears, 77
Earth, 3, 4
    diameter of, 4
    inside of, 46
    lowest places on, 41
    magnetic field around, 17
    and moon, 6, 11
    natural disasters on, 45
    tectonic plates on, 61
    youngest (newest) places on, 41
Earth sciences, 37–64
Earthquakes, 45
    and tsunami, 57
Ecology, 66
Ecosystems, 73, 74
    niches in, 89
    parts of, 88
    and species destruction, 90
Edison, Thomas, 17, 33, 36
Einstein, Albert, 18, 25
El Niño, 64

Electrical transformers, 18
Electric clocks, 32
Electric eels, 15
Electric mixer, 33
Electricity, 15, 16, 17, 30
Electromagnetic energy, 25
Electromagnetism, 20
Electrons, 13, 14, 15, 28
Elements, 11, 28
    and atoms, 13
    carbon, 12
    and inorganic chemistry, 23
    periodic table of, 29
    radioactive, 23
Elements, The (Euclid), 103
Elephant seals, 71
Elephant trees, 71
Elephants, 70, 71
Elevators, 33
Ellipse, 99
Elliptical galaxies, 7
Endangered species list, 91
Energy, 18, 30
Environmental change, 86
Eozoic era, 47
Epoch, 23
Equations, 97
Equatorial currents, 60
Equilateral triangles, 99
Era, 23
Eraser, 32
Estuary, 53, 55, 62
Eternity, 23
Euclid, 103, 104
Euclidean geometry, 103
Europe, 58
Evaporation, 58
Evolution, 32, 69, 86, 91
Exothermic heat, 26
Explorer I, 9
Explosion, 24
Extinction, 86
Eye glasses, 35
Eyes, 77

F

Factors, 97
Fahrenheit, Daniel, 26
Fahrenheit scale, 14, 26
Falcons, 72
Family, 68
Farnsworth, Philo, 33
Fats, 82
Fauna, 88

Fire alarm, 33
Fires, 26
    forest, 89
Fish, 67, 68, 72
Fjords, 53
Fleas, 72
Flight, 31
Flood, 45
Flora, 88
Florida Keys, Florida, 39
Flower, 67, 88
Fluorescent light, 25
Flush toilet, 33
Flying horse (Pegasus), 69
Fog, 52
Force, 19
Forces of nature, 20
Ford, Henry, 31
Forest fires, 45, 89
Ford Model T, 31
Fossey, Dian, 91
Fossil fuel plants, 30
Fractions, 94, 96
France
    in space, 9
Franklin, Benjamin, 15, 32, 69
Franklin stove, 32
Fresh water, 58, 59
Friction, 21, 26
Frogs, 73, 87
Frozen food, 33
Full moons, 34
Fulton, Robert, 32
Fungi kingdom, 66, 67
Fungus, 67
Fussell, Jacob, 33

G

Gabor, Denis, 33
Gagarin, Yuri, 9
Galaxies, 7
Galilee, Galileo, 10, 32, 34
Garbage, 90
Gases, 50
Gazelle, 72
Gemstones, 47
General Motors, 31
Genus, 68
Geography, 38
Geologic time, 47
Geologists, 48
Geology, 38
Geometry, 103
Geothermal plants, 30

Germain, Sophie, 103
Germs, 82, 92
Giant squid, 71
Ginsbay, Charles, 33
Glaciers, 45, 46
Glenn, John, 9
Goddard, Robert, 32
Gold, 28
Goliath spider, 71
Goodall, Jane, 92
Goodyear, Charles, 32, 36
Gorillas, 91
Gorillas in the Mist (Fossey), 91
Grant's gazelle, 72
Granymede, 4
Grass, 67, 86, 87
Gravity, 20, 31, 102
Great Basin Desert, 60
Great Lakes, 59
Great Northern Railroad, 32
Great Salt Lake Desert, 60
Grechi, Alfred, 33
Green ash tree, 70
Greenhouse warming, 74
Greenland, 43, 45
Greenwood, John, 32
Greyhounds, 72
Grizzly bear, 71
Ground water, 58
Gulf Stream, 57, 60
Gulfs, 53
Gum disease, 84
Gun powder, 35

H

Hail, 57
Hale, William, 32
Hale-Bopp comet, 28
Haley's comet, 28
Hamster, 73
Hawaii, 39, 41, 43
Hearing, 77
Hearing aid, 33
Heart, 75
Heart attack, 81
Heat, 26
Heinkel Co., 33
Heinz, Henry, 33
Helium, 28
Hepatitis, 80
Heredity, 92
Hertz measurements, 21
Hetch Hetchy Valley (California), 46
Hexagon, 98

Himalayan mountain range, 42
Holdren, Capel, 33
Holmes, Arthur, 48
Holographic images, 33
Horses, 87
Hottest places
    in U.S., 44
Hour, 23
Howard, Thomas, 32
Hubble, Edwin, 7
Human beings, 68
Human blood, 83
Human body, 78, 84
Humboldt Current, 60
Humidity, 50
Humus, 59
Hurricane, 45, 64
Hyaukutake comet, 28
Hydroelectric plants, 30
Hydrogen, 11, 23, 28, 29
Hyperbola, 99
Hypothesis, 24

I

Ice ages, 46, 57
Ice cream, 33
Ice storm, 45
Igneous rocks, 46, 47
Imaginary numbers, 94
Immune system, 82
Incisor teeth, 84
Indian Ocean, 44, 53, 56
Industrial activity
    pollution from, 90
Inertia, 19
Infections, 82
Infinity, 96
Inner ear, 77
Inorganic chemistry, 23
Insects, 67, 68, 72
International date line, 39
Inter-tidal zone, 61
Inventions, 32–33
Ionized air, 50
Ionosphere, 48
Iron, 11
Irrational numbers, 94
Irregular galaxies, 7
Islands, 43
Isosceles triangles, 99
Italy
    in space, 9

J

Japan Current, 60
Jeans, 33
Jelly fish, 73
Jet aircraft, 33
Jovian planets, 3
Julius Caesar, 22
Jupiter, 3, 4, 5, 6, 31
Jurassic Period, 47, 85

K

Keck I & Keck II (Hawaii), 10
Kelp, 61
Kelvin, Lord, 26
Kelvin scale, 14, 26
Ketchup, 33
Kettering, Charles, 31
Kingdoms, 66, 68
Koalas, 73
Kodiak (Alaska), 43
Kohoutek comet, 28
Komodo dragon lizard, 71
Kovalevsky, Sonya, 104

L

Lake of the Woods, Minnesota, 39
Lakes, 59
Lalande 21185, 10
Lambert Glacier (Antarctica), 45
Land snakes, 73
Landslides
    and tsunami, 57
Lasers, 21
Latitudes, 39
Lawn mowers, 32
Laws of probability, 103
Lead, 28
Leakey, Louis, 91, 92
Leap year, 22
Lemur, 73
Length, 102
Lenormand, L., 32
Lichen, 67
Life sciences, 65–92
Ligaments, 83
Light, 6, 21, 25
Light bulbs, 17, 33, 36
Light years, 10, 25
Lightning, 15, 32, 50
Lippersky, Hans, 10
Liquid Paper, 33
Litoral drift, 54

Liver, 80
Living organisms, 66, 67, 68, 74
Loam, 59
Lobster, 62
Logarithms, 104
Logging/lumber
    pollution from, 90
Longitudes, 39
Luminescent light, 25
Luyten 726-8, 10
Lymph system, 82

M

Macrophages, 82
Madagascar, 43
Magic squares, 98
Magnetic poles, 59
Magnetism, 16, 17
Mamenchisaurus, 84
Mammals, 62, 67, 68
Mammoth blue whales, 70
Mammoth Caves, Kentucky, 39
Manatee, 62
Mantle
    of Earth, 46
Marconi, Guglielmo, 33
Marconi, Ltd., 33
Marianas Trench, 56
Mars, 3, 4, 31
Mars, Francis, 33
Marsh, 59
Martin, 72
Mass, 19, 102
Mass extinction, 86
Matches, 32
Math, 93–104
Math puzzles, 97
Mathematicians, 102–4
Matter, 18, 19
McDonald, Richard, 33
McDonald's burgers, 33
McKensie River (Canada), 38
Measurements
    metric and U.S., 102
Medical science, 66
Mediterranean Sea, 44
Mendelyeev, Dimitri, 29
Mendol, Gregor, 93
Mercury, 3, 4, 31
Mermaids, 69
Mesozoic era, 47
Metamorphic rocks, 46, 47
Meteorology, 38
Meteors and meteorites, 5

Metric measurements, 102
Michelin Company, 31
Microsecond, 23
Microwave ovens, 33
Microwaves, 21, 25
Milk chocolate, 33
Milky Way, 7
Millennium, 23
Millisecond, 23
Mimeograph copying, 32
Minerals, 47, 82
Minute, 23
Mississippi/Missouri River, 38
Mist, 57
Mixtures, 29
Mojave Desert, 60
Molars, 84
Mold, 67
Molecules, 13
Mollusks, 63, 68
Moment, 23
Mongefosen Falls (Norway), 38
Mont Blanc (France), 42
Month, 22, 23
Moon, 11, 31, 34, 56
Moons, 6
Moss, 67
Moths, 87
Motor cycle, 33
Motorola Corporation, 33
Mount Cerro Aconcagua (Argentina), 42
Mount Everest (Asia), 42
Mount Foraler (Alaska), 42
Mount Jaya (Java) (Oceania), 42
Mount Kilimanjaro (Africa), 42
Mount McKinley (Alaska), 42
Mount St. Elias (Alaska), 42
Mountain peaks/ranges, 42, 43
Mu–mesons, 14
Municipal trash energy, 30
Muscles, 80
Mushrooms, 67
Mussels, 63
Mythical animals, 69

N

Nanoseconds, 23
Napier, John, 104
Napoleon, 103
Nasworthy, Frank, 33
Natural disasters, 45
Natural selection, 69
Negative numbers, 94

Neptune, 3, 4, 31
Nervous system, 76, 77
Nesmith, Bette, 33
Neurons, 76
Neutrinos, 14
Neutron stars, 8
Neutrons, 13, 14, 28
New Guinea, 43
New moons, 34
Newton, Isaac, 10, 20, 24, 102
Night, 51
Nile River (Africa), 38
Nitrogen, 11, 28, 50
North America, 58
North Pole, 59
North Sea, 53
North Star, 28
Noses, 77
Nuclear fission, 17
Nuclear fusion, 17
Nuclear power plants, 30
Nucleus, 79
    of atom, 14
Number system, 94
Nutrients, 82
Nutrition, 79
Nylon, 33

O

Ob River Delta (Russia), 55
Ocean, 44, 53, 58
    currents in, 60
    depths of, 56
    fish in, 73
    mammals in, 62
    plants in, 61
Ocean thermal energy, 30
Ocean tides
    and moon, 11
Oceanography, 38
Octagons, 98
Octopus, 63
Oil wells, 33
Opossum, 73
Oppenheimer, Robert, 9
Orange trees, 70
Order, 68
Organic chemistry, 23
Otis, Leon, 33
Oxygen, 28, 35, 50
Oysters, 63
Ozark Mountain Range, 43
Ozone, 63

P

Pacemakers, 75
Pacific Ocean, 44, 53, 56
Pagers, 33
Painted Desert, 60
Paleontology, 66
Paleozoic era, 47
Pallas, 5
Paper, 88
Paper clips, 33
Parabolas, 99
Parachutes, 32
Parallelograms, 99
Partial vacuum, 27
Pasta-making machine, 32
Pasteur, Louis, 93
Pasteurization process, 93
Peanut butter, 33
Pegasus (flying horse), 69
Pelorosaurus, 84
Penguins, 62
Pentagons, 98
Perfect numbers, 97
Periodic table of elements, 29
Perkins, Jacob, 32
Perky, Henry, 33
Pesticides, 74
Peter, Daniel, 33
Petro-chemical discharge, 74
Petroleum spills, 74
Ph, 12
Philippine Sea, 44, 53
Phoenix, 69
Phonograph, 36
Phylum, 68
Physical sciences, 1–36
Physics, 2, 18, 19, 35, 102
Phytoplankton, 61
Pi (π), 95
Pigs, 73
Planets, 3, 31
Plant kingdom, 66, 67
Plants, 61, 66, 69, 73
Plato, 104
Plimpton, J., 33
Pluto, 3, 4, 31
Plutonium, 23, 29
Poisonous things, 73
Polar facts, 59
Pollution, 90
Polonium, 35
Poluostrov (Kazakhstan), 41
Ponderosa pine tree, 70

Ponds, 59
Porpoises, 62
Postcards, 33
Post-it® notes, 33
Potassium, 48
Power, electric, 16
Power plants, 30
Praying mantis, 72
Precipitation, 57, 58
Pressure, 27
Priestly, Joseph, 32, 35
Prime numbers, 95
Prince of Wales (Alaska), 43
Probability, laws of, 103
Problem-solving (math), 101
Pronghorn antelopes, 72
Propane, 23
Prospect Creek (Alaska), 44
Protein, 82
Protons, 13, 14, 28
Proxima Centauri, 4, 10
Ptolomy (king of Egypt), 103
Puerto Rico, 43
Pulsars, 8
Pumps, 27
Pyramids, 101

Q

Qattara Depression (China), 41
Quadrilaterals, 99
Quarks, 14
Quoddy Head, Maine, 39

R

Race horses, 72
Radar, 33
Radiation, 6
Radio, 33
Radioactivity, 23, 35
Radium, 35
Railroads, 32
Rain, 39, 57, 64
Rainbows, 20, 51
Recessive traits (heredity), 92
Record players, 33
Recreation
    pollution from, 90
Rectangles, 98, 99
Recycling, 88
Red cedar trees, 70
Red deer, 72
Red Giants, 8
Red Sea, 53

Redwood trees, 70
Regency Electronics, 33
Regular shapes, 98
Renewable energy, 30
Reptiles, 67, 68
Reservoirs, 59
Resistance
    electric, 16
Rh factor, 83
Rheumatic fever, 82
Right triangles, 99
Rio Grande River (U.S.), 38
Rivers, 38, 58
Rockets, 24, 32
Rocks, 46, 48
Rocky Mountain Range, 43
Roentgen, Wilhelm, 33, 36
Roller skates, 33
Roman numerals, 96
Rubber tires, 32
Rumford, Count, 21, 26
Rutherford, Ernest, 14

S

Safety pins, 32
Sahara Desert, 60
Sailfish, 72
Salmon, 87
Salt, 13, 47, 55
Salton Sea (California), 41, 42
Salt-water crocodiles, 71
San Andreas fault line (California), 61
Sand bars, 54
Sand storms, 45
Sargasso seas, 53
Satellites, 6, 33
Saturn, 3, 4, 6, 31
Sauria, Charles, 32
Scalene triangles, 99
Scientific method, 24
Scorpions, 73, 78
Scotch tape, 33
SCUBA (self-contained underwater breathing
    apparatus), 54
Sea anemones, 73
Sea level
    places lower than, 41, 42
Sea lions, 62
Sea of Galilee, 53
Sea of Japan, 53
Sea otters, 62
Sea snakes, 73
Seals, 62
Seas, 44, 53

Seasons, 23
Second, 23
Sedimentary rocks, 46, 47
Seismosaurus, 84
Semi-conductors, 18
Sequoia trees, 70
Sewing machines, 32
Shapes, 98, 99
Sharks, 72
Shooting stars, 5
Showers, 57
Shrimp, 62
Siberian tigers, 71
Sierra Mountain Range, 43
Sierra Nevada Mountains, 46
Silly Putty®, 33
Silver, 28
Silver, Spencer, 33
Silver maple trees, 70
Single cell kingdoms, 66, 67
Sirius, 10
Skateboards, 33
Skeletal muscles, 80
Skeleton (human), 83
Skin, 79
Skull, 83
Sky, 51
Sleep, 81
Sleet, 57
Sloth, 73
Smog, 74
Smooth muscles, 80
Snails, 63
Snakes, 73
Snider, Jacob, 33
Snow, 51, 57
Sodium, 28
Soil, 59
Solar energy, 30
Solar systems
    size of planets in, 4
Solar wind, 6
Sony Corporation, 33
Sound, 21, 25, 77
South America, 58
South China Sea, 44, 53
South Pole, 59
Southern Hemisphere currents, 60
Space
    animals in, 9
Space dust, 6
Space travel
    first countries in, 9
Species, 68
    extinction of, 86

Speed, 104
Spencer, Percy, 33
Sperm whale, 71
Spiders, 67, 68, 73, 78
Spiral galaxies, 7
Spring tides, 56
Springbok, 72
Sputnik I, 9, 33
Squares, 99
Squids, 63
Squirrels, 73
St. Lawrence River (Canada), 38
Stainless steel, 33
Stalactites, 41
Stalagmites, 41
Stanley brothers, 31
Stanley Steamer, 31
Stars, 7, 8, 10, 28
Static electricity, 15
Steam engine, 32
Steam heat, 32
Steamships, 32
Stethoscopes, 33
Stirrup bone (middle ear), 83
Straits, 53
Stratosphere, 48
Stratus clouds, 49
Strauss, Levi, 33
Streams, 58
Strokes, 81
Strong force, 20
Studebaker, 33
Submarines, 32
Sub-phylum, 68
Substances, 13
Sugar, 23
Sulfur, 50
Sun, 2
    distance from planets to, 3
Sunrise, 51
Sunset, 51
Supernovas, 8
Supersaurus, 84
Surface water, 58
Surreal numbers, 94
Surtsey Island, 41
Survival of the fittest, 69
Swamps, 59
Swan, Joseph, 17
Swifts, 72
Swim fins, 32
Sycamore trees, 70

T

Tadpoles, 87
Tapeworms, 71
Tasman Sea, 53
Tau-mesons, 14
T-cells, 82
Tectonic plates, 61
Teeth, 84
Telephones, 30, 33
Telescopes, 10, 32, 34
Television, 33
Temperature, 26
Temperature scales, 14, 26
Terrestrial planets, 3
Teton Mountain Range, 43
Thesis, 24
Thomson, R., 32
Thorium, 23
Three-toed sloths, 72
Thunder, 51
Tides, 56
Time, 21
    geologic, 47
    terms for, 23
Timonnier, Barthelemy, 32
Tires, 32
Titan
    moon of, 4
Tomato ketchup, 33
Tornadoes, 45, 63
Torricelli, 49
Toxic dumping, 74
Trace elements in air, 50
Traffic lights, 33
Transformers, electrical, 18
Transistor radios, 33
Trapezoids, 99
Trees, 67, 70, 71, 88
Trevithick, Richard, 31
Triangles, 98, 99, 100
Triassic Period, 47, 85
Tributary, 58
Tropic of Cancer, 45
Tropic of Capricorn, 45
Troposhpere, 48
Tsiolkovsky, Konstantin, 32
Tsunamis, 45, 57
Tucker, S., 33
Tugela Falls (South Africa), 38
Tupper, Earl, 33
Tupperware, 33
Turfan Depression (China), 41

TV ads, 33
Twisters, 63
Typhoons, 64

U

Ultrasaurus, 84
Unicorns, 69
United States
    deserts in, 60
    major estuaries in, 55
    mountain ranges in (major), 43
    snowiest cities in, 51
    in space, 9
    trees in, 70
    windiest cities in, 52
Universal Company, 33
Universe, 2, 6
Unununium, 11
Uranium, 23, 28, 35
Uranus, 3, 4, 31
Utlgard Falls (Norway), 38

V

Vacuum, 27
Vacuum cleaner, 27
Vasler, Johann, 33
Velocity, 19
Venus, 3, 4, 31
Vesta, 5
Video games, 33
Video tapes, 33
Viruses, 66, 82
Vitamins, 79, 82
Volcanoes, 45
Voltage, 16
Volume
    finding, 101
    measurements of, 100, 102
Vulcanized rubber, 32, 36

W

Walkman, 33
Walrus, 62
Walsh, Alan, 33
Wang, An, 33, 101
War of 1812, 32
Washing machines, 33
Washington state
    mountain ranges in, 42
Water, 12, 13, 29
    and temperature scales, 14
Water cycle, 58
Water spouts, 63
Water vapor, 50

Waterfalls, 38
Watson, James, 81
Watt, James, 32
Waves, 55, 56
WBNT (New York), 33
Weak force, 20
    and radioactivity, 23
Weather-related natural disasters, 45
Weeds, 67, 87
Week, 23
Weight, 19, 31
Whale shark, 71
Whales, 62, 70
White blood cells, 82
White dwarfs, 8
White Sands Desert, 60
Whitney, Eli, 32
Whole frequency spectrum, 21
Whole numbers, 94
Williston, William, 32
Willow trees, 70
Wilson, Walter, 33
Wind, 52
Wind energy, 30
Wisdom teeth, 84
Wist, Frederick, 32
Wolf 359, 10
Wolves, 90
Word processors, 33, 101
Work, 19
Worms, 67, 68
Wright, James, 33
Wright brothers, 33
Wyman, Arthur, 33

X

Xerox, 33
X-rays, 25, 33, 36

Y

Yangtze River (China), 38
Year, 22, 23
    on planets, 4
Yellow River (China), 38
Yellow Sea, 53
Yenisey River (Eurasia), 38
Yosemite Falls (California), 38
Yosemite Valley (California), 46
Yukon River (Alaska), 38

Z

Zebras, 87
Zero, 94, 104
Zinc, 28

TV ads, 33
Twisters, 63
Typhoons, 64

U

Ultrasaurus, 84
Unicorns, 69
United States
    deserts in, 60
    major estuaries in, 55
    mountain ranges in (major), 43
    snowiest cities in, 51
    in space, 9
    trees in, 70
    windiest cities in, 52
Universal Company, 33
Universe, 2, 6
Unununium, 11
Uranium, 23, 28, 35
Uranus, 3, 4, 31
Utlgard Falls (Norway), 38

V

Vacuum, 27
Vacuum cleaner, 27
Vasler, Johann, 33
Velocity, 19
Venus, 3, 4, 31
Vesta, 5
Video games, 33
Video tapes, 33
Viruses, 66, 82
Vitamins, 79, 82
Volcanoes, 45
Voltage, 16
Volume
    finding, 101
    measurements of, 100, 102
Vulcanized rubber, 32, 36

W

Walkman, 33
Walrus, 62
Walsh, Alan, 33
Wang, An, 33, 101
War of 1812, 32
Washing machines, 33
Washington state
    mountain ranges in, 42
Water, 12, 13, 29
    and temperature scales, 14
Water cycle, 58
Water spouts, 63
Water vapor, 50

Waterfalls, 38
Watson, James, 81
Watt, James, 32
Waves, 55, 56
WBNT (New York), 33
Weak force, 20
    and radioactivity, 23
Weather-related natural disasters, 45
Weeds, 67, 87
Week, 23
Weight, 19, 31
Whale shark, 71
Whales, 62, 70
White blood cells, 82
White dwarfs, 8
White Sands Desert, 60
Whitney, Eli, 32
Whole frequency spectrum, 21
Whole numbers, 94
Williston, William, 32
Willow trees, 70
Wilson, Walter, 33
Wind, 52
Wind energy, 30
Wisdom teeth, 84
Wist, Frederick, 32
Wolf 359, 10
Wolves, 90
Word processors, 33, 101
Work, 19
Worms, 67, 68
Wright, James, 33
Wright brothers, 33
Wyman, Arthur, 33

X

Xerox, 33
X-rays, 25, 33, 36

Y

Yangtze River (China), 38
Year, 22, 23
    on planets, 4
Yellow River (China), 38
Yellow Sea, 53
Yenisey River (Eurasia), 38
Yosemite Falls (California), 38
Yosemite Valley (California), 46
Yukon River (Alaska), 38

Z

Zebras, 87
Zero, 94, 104
Zinc, 28

The Science and Math Bookmark Book